PROPHETIC INSIGHTS FOR DAILY LIVING

VOLUME 3

~~

Inspired Messages From The Holy Spirit

Sheila Eismann

Books by Sheila Eismann

A STORMY YEAR – BOOK 2 OF THE SABBLONTI SERIES

A WOMAN OF SUBSTANCE – A 12-WEEK BIBLE STUDY

CREATIVE AUTHORS' WORKBOOK JOURNAL – A STEP-BY-STEP GUIDE FOR YOUR WRITING EXPERIENCE

HEART TO HEART FROM GOD'S WORD

LOVE, THE TIE THAT BINDS – BOOK 3 OF THE SABBLONTI SERIES

JANTZI'S JOKERS – BOOK 1 OF THE SABBLONTI SERIES

POETRY TIME – VOLUME ONE

PROPHETIC INSIGHTS FOR DAILY LIVING – MESSAGES INSPIRED BY THE HOLY SPIRIT – VOLUME 1

PROPHETIC INSIGHTS FOR DAILY LIVING – MESSAGES INSPIRED BY THE HOLY SPIRIT – VOLUME 2

PROPHETIC INSIGHTS FOR DAILY LIVING – MESSAGES INSPIRED BY THE HOLY SPIRIT – VOLUME 3

RECOGNIZE YOUR CIRCLES

STIRRINGS OF THE SPIRIT

STRAIGHT FROM THE HORSE'S TROUGH

THE CHRISTMAS TIN

Copyright © 2021 by Sheila Eismann.

www.sheilaeismann.com

All rights reserved. No portion of this book may be reproduced, stored in a retrieval system, or transmitted in any form or by any means — electronic, mechanical, photocopy, recording, scanning, or other — except for brief quotations in critical reviews or articles, without the prior written permission of the publisher.

Published by Desert Sage Press
www.desertsagepress.com

Printed and bound in the United States of America.

Cover design by Cathie Richardson. **www.countrygardenstitchery.com**
All rights reserved.

Any trademarks, service marks, product names, or named features are used only for reference, are assumed to be the property of their respective owners, and the use of any one of those terms does not imply an endorsement on the part of the author and/or the publisher.

ISBN: 978-1-7373135-2-6

Library of Congress Control Number: 2021919188

Scripture taken from the New King James Version. Copyright 1979, 1980, 1982 by Thomas Nelson, Inc. Used by permission. All rights reserved.

Scripture quotations marked (NIV) are taken from the Holy Bible, New International Version®, NIV®. Copyright © 1973, 1978, 1984, 2011 by Biblica, Inc.® Used by permission of Zondervan. All rights reserved worldwide. www.zondervan.com. The "NIV" and "New International Version" are trademarks registered in the United States Patent and Trademark Office by Biblica, Inc.®

DEDICATION

    This series of workbooks is dedicated to my beloved husband, Dan, who our precious grandkiddos affectionately refer to as "Poppy." He's my best friend, confidant, loyal companion, and fellow believer in our Lord and Savior, Jesus Christ. I will be forever grateful for God knitting our hearts together in His love and giving us compatible and mutually beneficial spiritual giftings.

    We've experienced challenges, supreme blessings, miracles, and victories during the 38 years of our marriage. God has sustained us every single day and step of the way by His mighty right hand, His beloved Son, Jesus Christ, The Holy Spirit, His Word, and His ministering angels.

    We're eternally grateful for all of the divine appointments God has orchestrated with those of His choosing throughout the intersections of our lives.

    It's been the honor and privilege of a lifetime to walk side-by-side with Dan as we continue to learn, laugh, and love together. To God be the glory, both now and forevermore!

ACKNOWLEDGEMENTS

My heartfelt gratitude, sincere appreciation, and blessings are extended to Cathie Richardson, Lesta Chadez, and Marilyn Battisti for their invaluable assistance and encouragement in publishing this set of prophetic workbooks.

It's been a special joy to share this experience with my oldest daughter, Cathie, whose artistic gifts and talents bless me beyond measure. For a real treat, please check out her website: **www.countrygardenstitchery.com**

Fifty-three years ago, Lesta and I lived in the same small rural area. Our paths reconnected at just the right time. Despite navigating her own set of life's challenges, Lesta's dynamic combination of mercy and exhortation is a bonus for any writer. In addition, she's a poet, author, and spiritual songwriter.

Being a retired school teacher, Marilyn operates from a unique vantage point with respect to almost everything she reads and studies, especially as it relates to spiritual matters. I continue to be amazed when reading her thoughts if she opts to post a comment on my website after I've authored one of my blog posts! Since Marilyn has a real heart for intercessory prayer, she's blessed my life immensely as a prayer partner.

In addition, I want to thank my Lord Jesus for helping me every day in every way. With Him, all things are possible. (Matthew 19:26) I'm grateful for The Holy Spirit and His gifts of creativity which are inherent within each of us in various forms.

TABLE OF CONTENTS

Introduction	13
Our Sphere of Authority	27
Growing In Hope – Petal # 1	34
Growing In Hope – Petal # 2	42
Growing In Hope – Petal # 3	50
Growing In Hope – Petal # 4	58
The New, Big Bend In The River Of Your Life	65
Growing In Hope – Petal # 5	73
Growing In Hope – Petal # 6	81
Growing In Hope – Petal # 7	89
Growing In Hope – Petal # 8	98
The Coyote, Peter & Summer	108
Be Filled & Poured Out!	118
Drink From Wisdom's Cup	127
The Covenant Academy on Deuteronomy Street	138
Blessed Are The Flexible	148
Like A Tree Planted By The Waters	156
The Woman and The Candle	165
Your Rest Will Be Your Reset	174
4 Keys To Open 4 Doors	185
Light, Grace & The Yellow Roses	195
Supernatural Sights & Sounds	203

About The Author 213

Other Books Available from Sheila Eismann, Dan Eismann & Desert Sage Press 215

Notes and Reflections 221

FOREWARD

Woven into the fabric of our lives wherein a silver cord is intertwined throughout the tapestry, there are people in our circle of friends where our hearts are bound together through the Holy Spirit. Sheila Eismann is a special friend that God has placed in my life as the Lord has knit our hearts together in His love. We grew up in the same rural town, and our parents were friends. From this friendship, a bond of love was birthed.

As I have read Sheila's books and followed her writings and blogs over the years, her prophetic visions and dreams have ministered to me in many areas. I give praise to our Lord and Savior Jesus Christ for the many ways He has been with me throughout my life. The Lord especially filled my heart with a living hope through a time of testing when my husband entered into his eternal home in 2019. Special friends like Sheila prayed for me through this difficult journey, and I will be forever grateful for the many ways the Lord has strengthened me and given me hope.

Sheila has a gifting and unique way of weaving in words of wisdom, encouragement, and exhortation as she shares with us what the Lord has given her in visions, dreams, and prophetic words. When we face times of trouble, testing, or tribulation, she has a way of bringing her messages to a practical application in our daily lives by sharing words of comfort and hope while challenging us to pursue a deeper walk with the Lord.

The prophetic visions and dreams the Lord has shared with Sheila are for anyone who wants a fresh infusion of faith and strength to start each day. They are for those walking through difficult seasons of life such as loneliness, grief, or change. The wisdom the Lord shares with her may be for those who are overwhelmed by life's challenges and for those who may be concerned about loved ones or the condition of the world around us. When it seems like the circumstances of life and the storms that surround us are pulling us under, she reminds us that the Lord is the Victor and encourages us to continue to put our trust and hope in Him as He is faithful and true to His promises and His Holy Word.

Every day we need wisdom and fresh insight as we walk out the fullness of our salvation in our journey through this earthly life. The workbooks that Sheila has prepared can be as a devotional and also used in a Bible study. Her prophetic writings will be a blessing to those who have open hearts ready to receive what the Lord has for them.

Lesta Chadez, Poet, Spiritual Song Writer, and Author of *Treasures Hidden In Plain Sight, A Collection of Poems and Short Stories.*

You will be ever so blessed to read the prophetic articles by Sheila Eismann. Each of her visions is a timely message to guide and direct you in your everyday living. Having the inspiration from The Holy Spirit, each of Sheila's writings is a direct appointment for you to individually meet with our Lord Jesus and find manna for your soul. Sheila's prophetic visions will definitely inspire you and lift you to another level of Christianity!

Marilyn Battisti, Retired Educator

INTRODUCTION

Prophetic Insights For Daily Living was written with you, the spiritual seeker, Bible reader, and student, in mind to render assistance regarding spiritual gifts, dreams, visions, and prophetic words.

To introduce this new series of workbooks, I deem it's important to go into greater detail concerning the three revelatory gifts of the Holy Spirit listed in 1 Corinthians 12:4-11. These gifts are the word of wisdom, the word of knowledge, and the discerning of spirits.

"There are diversities of gifts, but the same Spirit. There are differences of ministries, but the same Lord. And there are diversities of activities, but it is the same God who works all in all. But the manifestation of the Spirit is given to each one for the profit *of all:* **for to one is given the word of wisdom through the Spirit, to another the word of knowledge through the same Spirit**, to another faith by the same Spirit, to another gifts of healings by the same Spirit, to another the working of miracles, to another prophecy, **to another discerning of spirits**, to another *different* kinds of tongues, to another the interpretation of tongues. But one and the same Spirit works all these things, distributing to each one individually as He wills." [Emphasis mine]

Writing to the church at Corinth, Paul said, "Now concerning spiritual *gifts*, brethren, I do not want you to be ignorant:" [1 Corinthians 12:1]

During its establishment phase, God did not want the church in Corinth to be ignorant concerning these matters, and His desire is no less for present-day churches or Bible-believing Christians.

An important aspect to remember is the Holy Spirit distributes His gifts to each one individually as He wills. [1 Corinthians 12:11] Every single one of the spiritual gifts outlined in 1 Corinthians 12:4-10 is precisely just that, a gift which cannot be bought, traded, manufactured, contrived, manipulated, or you fill in the blank.

<u>The Holy Spirit gift of the word of wisdom and the gift of the word of knowledge:</u>

"Before we begin our study of the gifts of the Holy Spirit, it is important for us to understand that in the scriptures there is a mingling of gifts, so much so that at times we may question just which gift (or gifts) is being manifested. This need cause us no real concern, for it must be remembered that all of the gifts flow from the same source, The Holy Spirit. If we are unable to identify exactly and classify perfectly, let us not be overly concerned. As humans, it is our nature to draw neat lines of separation and classification, but when we seek to impose this practice upon God, we only frustrate ourselves, and we may generate unnecessary confusion.

The word of wisdom and the word of knowledge are two gifts that often work together. Throughout the Old Testament when the prophets would prophesy, the word of wisdom and the word of knowledge would flow together (knowledge, and what to do about it.) In reading the prophetic books of the Old Testament, you will notice the phrase time and time again, "The WORD of the Lord came to _____ (name)." Examples of this can be found in 1 Kings 17:8; Jeremiah 1:4-8; Ezekiel 1:3; Joel 1:1 and Haggai 1:1.

In the New Testament, much of the writings of Paul, Peter, James, and Jude are the word of wisdom and word of knowledge. Also, John's letters to the churches in Revelation chapters 2-3 are this mixture. The word of wisdom often comes with the word of knowledge so that believers in Christ will know how to apply that knowledge correctly. These gifts are two of the three gifts that 'reveal' something. We call these gifts revelation gifts because they consist of information supernaturally revealed from God. Each of these gifts is the God-given ability to receive from Him facts concerning something, anything, about which it is humanly impossible for us to know, revealed to the believer so that he or she may be protected, pray more effectively, or help someone in need.

The gift of the word of knowledge is supernatural in character. It is not obtained by logic, or deduction, reasoning, etc., or by natural senses, but by supernatural revelation through The Holy Spirit. It is the sheer gift of God. It is not essentially a vocal gift. It is received quietly and inaudibly within the person's spirit. It may become vocal when shared with others.

A basic definition of the word of knowledge: a fragment or small item of God's knowledge, supernaturally revealed to a person by The Holy Spirit.

An example of a spoken word of knowledge can be found in John 1:47-49:

'Jesus saw Nathanael coming toward Him, and said of him, 'Behold, an Israelite indeed, in whom is no deceit!'

Nathanael said to Him, 'How do You know me?'

Jesus answered and said to him, 'Before Philip called you, when you were under the fig tree, I saw you.'

Nathanael answered and said to Him, 'Rabbi, You are the Son of God! You are the King of Israel!'

It is important to consider what the word of knowledge is not:

- It is not human knowledge gained by natural means.

- It is not human knowledge sanctified by God.

- It cannot be gained by intellectual learning, studying books, or pursuing academics.

- It is not the ability to study, understand, or interpret the Bible.

- It is not a psychic phenomenon or extra-sensory perception such as telepathy (the supposed ability to be able to read minds), clairvoyance (the supposed ability to know things that are happening elsewhere), or precognition (the supposed ability to know the future.)

The gifts of the Spirit defy human scientific explanation and are not acquired by ordinary educational processes. No amount of education or learning can produce them. They are not dependent upon innate human qualities. For example, the word of wisdom might be spoken by a person or even less than ordinary wisdom. They are not accentuated natural talents and abilities. The least talented or able may as likely be the agent through whom God works as the most intellectually endowed.

It is a subtle ploy of the great deceiver of our souls to attempt to humanize the supernatural and to reduce the spiritual gifts to the level of mere human endowments, talents, and learned or acquired abilities.

A word of knowledge may be revealed to a believer in any of the following ways:

- A sudden inspiration or a deep inner impression.

- A dream, vision, or picture seen through the eye of the spirit, with the interpretation of what is seen.

- Hearing the voice of God, or of angels, audibly or in the ear of the spirit.

- A living personal word from the Lord through scripture.

- The vocal gifts of the Holy Spirit such as tongues, interpretation of tongues, or prophecy. [1 Corinthians 12:10]

Supernatural visions and dreams are usually the word of wisdom or word of knowledge in operation. Acts 2:17-18 reminds us of what was spoken by the prophet Joel,

> *'And it shall come to pass in the last days, says God,*
> *That I will pour out of My Spirit on all flesh;*
> *Your sons and your daughters shall prophesy,*
> *Your young men shall see visions,*
> *Your old men shall dream dreams.*
> *And on My menservants and on My maidservants*
> *I will pour out My Spirit in those days;*
> *And they shall prophesy.'*

The word of knowledge may not always be fully understood by the receiver or the hearers. It can seem like it's a riddle or a mystery. In the seventh and eighth chapters of the book of Daniel, we read where the prophet was troubled in his spirit, and the visions that were given to him disturbed him greatly. In Daniel 8:27b, God's servant was appalled by the vision, and it was beyond his understanding.

Oftentimes God will use a word of knowledge to uncover sin, bring people to Him, give guidance and direction, minister encouragement or impart knowledge of future events. Some Bible scholars teach the revelation of future events to be the gift of the word of wisdom rather than the word of knowledge since wisdom usually pertains to what to do in the future.

If you would like to take the time to examine some examples of a word of knowledge in the Bible, I have listed a few from the Old Testament and the New Testament.

Old Testament:

- 1 Samuel 3:10-14
- 1 Samuel 10:17-23
- 1 Kings 19:11-18
- 2 Kings 5:20-27
- 2 Kings 6:8-23

New Testament:

- Luke 2:25-26

- John 1:29-34
- John 6:60-61
- John 13:38
- Acts 5:1-11

Hosea 4:6a reminds us that God's people are destroyed for lack of knowledge. We definitely need the gift of the word of knowledge operating in our lives and churches today!

The word of wisdom is a flash of inspiration. It is a supernatural revelation sufficient for the occasion of the wisdom or purpose of God. It is the wisdom needed to meet a particular situation, or answer a particular question, or utilize a particular piece of information.

Once again, it is vital to consider what the word of wisdom is and is not:

- It is not natural wisdom.
- It is not the wisdom gained from academic achievement.
- It is not wisdom gained from experience.
- It is not even the wisdom to understand the Bible.
- It is given as the Holy Spirit wills (1 Corinthians 12:11).
- It is given for a specific need or situation.

A word of wisdom may be revealed to a believer in Christ the same way that I have listed previously for the word of knowledge.

It is helpful to know that we can pray for wisdom, understanding, and knowledge. In Ephesians 1:17, Paul prayed for the spirit of wisdom and revelation. In Colossians 1:9, Paul asked God to fill the believers in the church in Colosse with the knowledge of His will in all wisdom and spiritual understanding.

The following are examples of a word of wisdom found in the Old Testament and the New Testament:

Old Testament:

- Genesis 6:13-21

- Genesis 41:33 with Acts 7:10
- Exodus 28:3; 31:6 and 35:26
- Judges 7:5
- 2 Samuel 5:17-25

New Testament:

- Matthew 2:12-15
- Matthew 21:23-27
- Luke 20:22-26
- John 8:3-7
- Acts 27:23-26[i]

The Holy Spirit gift of discerning of spirits:

"The third gift along with the word of wisdom and word of knowledge that reveals something is the gift of discerning of spirits. It has a narrower range than the other two because it is limited to the spirit world.

Sometimes this gift has been called the gift of discernment which is in error. It is the gift of discerning of spirits. It is not the gift of discerning people; it is the gift of discerning of spirits. There is a huge difference.

From our study of scripture, we learn that there are four basic categories of spirits in the spirit world which are as follows:

- God - John 4:24
- Angels – Hebrews 1:14
- Evil spirits, deceiving spirits and demons - Ephesians 6:12; 1 Timothy 4:1 and Revelation 16:14
- Man - Zechariah 12:1; 1 Corinthians 2:11a

A believer in Christ may be (1) operating under the inspiration of the Holy Spirit; or (2) expressing his or her own thoughts, feelings, and desires from his or her soul or spirit; or (3) allowing an alien spirit to oppress him or her and be bringing thoughts from that wrong spirit. An unbeliever in Christ may be completely possessed by an evil spirit. (Luke 8:26-39) The gift of discerning of spirits immediately reveals what is taking place. This gift is given to know what is in a person and to know the spirit that motivates him or her.

First, we need to define the word 'discern.' It is looking beyond the outward to the inward, literally, 'seeing right through', or 'insight.' In the gift of discerning of spirits, it means to distinguish between good and evil spiritual influences.

The following three verses are a sample of how the word 'discern' is used in the Bible:

- 2 Samuel 14:17 – 'And now your servant [the woman from Tekoa] says, 'May the word of my lord the king bring me rest, for my lord the king is like an angel of God in discerning good and evil. May the LORD your God be with you.' [NIV]

- 2 Samuel 19:35a – 'I [Barzillai the Gileadite] *am* today eighty years old. Can I discern between the good and bad?'

- Ezekiel 44:23 – 'And they [the priests] shall teach My people *the difference* between the holy and the unholy, and cause them to discern between the unclean and the clean.'

Some Biblical scholars believe that if there are no visions, (actually **seeing** the spirit), it is not the gift of discerning of spirits, but rather the gift of the word of knowledge in operation. They reason that if one is informed about a spirit, but has no vision of the spirit, he or she would not **discern** it. In some cases, a WORD comes first, then a vision follows.

Through the gift of discerning of spirits, we can discern the origin of certain actions, teachings, and circumstances that have been inspired by spiritual beings. It is the ability given by God to know what spirit is motivating a person or situation. The gift allows a believer to detect and identify spirits and provides supernatural revelation of the unseen spirit world, both good and evil. The real nature of this gift is knowing and judging – never guessing.

The gift of discerning of spirits is not a natural critical spirit, insight into human nature, human shrewdness, character reading, fault-finding, psychological insight or even spiritual discernment. It is not a spiritual gift to uncover human failings. It is not the spirits of people who have died. It has nothing to do with spiritism or spiritualism. The spirits of departed human beings are not on this earth and to attempt to contact them is forbidden. [Deuteronomy 18:9-12]

Discerning of spirits is needed primarily to reveal the source of spirits. The first and most obvious function of this gift is to reveal the presence of evil spirits in the lives of people or churches. However, it also functions to evaluate the source of a prophetic message, a particular teaching, or some supernatural manifestation. The person functioning with this gift will be able to tell whether the source of the message or act is demonic, divine, or merely human. The gift of discerning of spirits enables a Christian to pick out the source of gifts and messages that truly come from God. Humans cannot be in contact with or understand the spiritual realm except by the power of God or the power of Satan. (1 Corinthians 2:14)

Although the gift has to do primarily with evil spirits, it also is the ability to detect the presence of the Holy Spirit. Visions, seeing Jesus or angels are also included in the discerning of spirits. If one only discerns evil spirits, then the Holy Spirit gift of discerning of spirits is not in operation.

Our natural discernment can be easily fooled. The gift of discerning of spirits is a means of protection from satanic deception. It is easy to confuse the words of the spirit of Satan with those of the Spirit of God. Satan counterfeits the beautiful works of God by creating an outward appearance that is similar to the real work of the Holy Spirit.

Satan is known as the deceiver [Revelation 12:9], the father of lies [John 8:44], and the serpent [Revelation 20:2]. All these titles signify the subtle, crafty deceptiveness which he uses to bring about evil whenever he can. Many times, his counterfeit is so plausible that one will be entirely deceived unless someone is present who functions with the supernatural gift of discerning of spirits. If demon activity was always so obviously reeking with evil and wicked intent, as we tend to imagine, there would no use for this gift of the Holy Spirit."[ii]

The following are examples of discerning of spirits found in the Old Testament and the New Testament:

Old Testament:

- Genesis 21:17-19

- Leviticus 19:31

- Deuteronomy 32:17

- Judges 13:3-7

- 1 Samuel 16:14-15, 23
- 1 Samuel 28:11-19
- 1 Kings 19:5-8
- 2 Kings 6:17
- 2 Chronicles 18:18-22
- Zechariah 3:1-2

New Testament:
- Matthew 1:20-21
- Matthew 16:23
- Luke 1:11-20; 26-38
- Luke 13:11, 16
- Acts 12:7-10
- Acts 13:9-11
- Acts 27:23-24
- 1 John 4:1"

Despite teachings to the contrary, God's people do receive dreams, visions, and prophetic words today. Here's a basic overview of this aspect of the revelatory realm:

1. God communicates through His prophets in one of two ways. "Let the prophet who has a dream tell the dream, but let him who has my word speak my word faithfully."iii As an aside, why would God want to stop communicating to us through prophets? Has He stopped speaking? Do people no longer need to hear from Him?

2. *Nābiy' * prophet. One of the ways God communicates to us is through a *nābiy'* prophet. "This word describes one who was raised up by God and, as such, could only proclaim that which the Lord gave him to say. A prophet could not contradict the Law of the Lord or speak from his own mind or heart."[iv] "I [God] will raise up for them a prophet [*nābiy'*] like you [Moses] from among their brothers. And I will put my words in his mouth, and he shall speak to them all that I command him."[v] Jeremiah was a *nābiy'* prophet, and he tried to refrain from giving the word of the Lord because doing so made him "a reproach and derision all day long."[vi] However, he could not refrain from giving the word of God.

> If I say, "I will not mention him,
>   or speak any more in his name,"
> there is in my heart as it were a burning fire
>   shut up in my bones,
> and I am weary with holding it in,
>   and I cannot.[vii]

3. *Hōzeh* prophets. Another way that God communicates to us is through a *hōzeh* or *chōzeh* prophet (hereinafter *hōzeh* prophet). "The word is "[a] masculine noun meaning a seer, prophet. ... The word means one who sees or perceives; it is used in parallel with the participle of the verb that means literally to see, to perceive. ... It appears that the participles of *hōzeh* and *rā'āh* function synonymously. But, terminology aside, a seer functioned the same as a prophet, who was moved by God and had divinely given insight."[viii] *Rā'āh* or *rō'eh* is "a verb meaning to see" and can "connote a spiritual observation and comprehension by means of seeing visions."[ix]

A prophet can function as both a *nābiy'* prophet and a *hōzeh* prophet. For example, Jeremiah functioned as both.

> But the Lord said to me,
>   "Do not say, 'I am only a youth';
>   for to all to whom I send you, you shall go,
>   and whatever I command you, you shall speak.
>   . . . .
>   declares the Lord."
> Then the Lord put forth His hand and touched my mouth, and the Lord said to me:
>   "Behold, I have put My words in your mouth.
>   . . . .
>   And the word of the Lord came to me, saying, "Jeremiah, what do you see?" And I said, "I see an almond branch." Then the Lord said to me, "You have seen well, for I am watching over my word to perform it."[x]

King David was assigned all three types of prophets.

> Now the acts of King David, from first to last, are written in the Chronicles of Samuel the seer [*rā'āh*], and in the Chronicles of Nathan the

prophet [nāḇiy'], and in the Chronicles of Gad the seer [hōzeh], with accounts of all his rule and his might and of the circumstances that came upon him and upon Israel and upon all the kingdoms of the countries.[xi]

4. Examples of the ministry of prophets include the following:

   a. Rebuking someone for sin.

      The LORD sent Nathan the prophet to David to tell him a story about a rich man who stole and prepared for eating a lamb that had been raised in the home of a poor man.[xii]

      Then David's anger was greatly kindled against the man, and he said to Nathan, "As the LORD lives, the man who has done this deserves to die, and he shall restore the lamb fourfold, because he did this thing, and because he had no pity."[xiii]

      Nathan then said to David "You are the man!" referring to David having Uriah the Hittite killed in battle in order to cover the sin of David's adultery with Bathsheba.[xiv]

   b. Turning peoples' hearts to the LORD.

      An angel appeared to Zechariah and told him that Elizabeth, his wife who was barren and advanced in years, would have a child, "[a]nd he [John the Baptist] will turn many of the children of Israel to the Lord their God."[xv]

   c. Bringing people back into a covenant relationship with God.

      And they abandoned the house of the LORD, the God of their fathers, and served the Asherim and the idols. And wrath came upon Judah and Jerusalem for this guilt of theirs. Yet he sent prophets among them to bring them back to the LORD. These testified against them, but they would not pay attention.[xvi]

   d. Warning of what will occur in the future.

      Now in these days prophets came down from Jerusalem to Antioch. And one of them named Agabus stood up and foretold by the Spirit that there would be a great famine over all the world (this took place in the days of Claudius). So the disciples determined, everyone according to his ability, to send relief to the brothers living in Judea. And they did so, sending it to the elders by the hand of Barnabas and Saul.[xvii]

   e. Exhorting and strengthening the brethren.

And Judas and Silas, who were themselves prophets, encouraged and strengthened the brothers with many words.[xviii]

f. Giving divine direction.

Now there were in the church at Antioch prophets and teachers, Barnabas, Simeon who was called Niger, Lucius of Cyrene, Manaen a lifelong friend of Herod the tetrarch, and Saul. While they were worshiping the Lord and fasting, the Holy Spirit said, "Set apart for me Barnabas and Saul for the work to which I have called them." Then after fasting and praying they laid their hands on them and sent them off.[xix]

g. Speaking against sin; warning of judgment, and preaching about hope and renewal.

Then the Lord put out his hand and touched my mouth. And the Lord said to me,
> "Behold, I have put my words in your mouth.
> See, I have set you this day over nations and over kingdoms,
> to pluck up and to break down,
> to destroy and to overthrow,
> to build and to plant."[xx]

Jeremiah's message is threefold: (1) he must **pluck up** and **break down**, which refers to preaching against sin; (2) he must **destroy** and **overthrow**, which relates to messages concerning judgment; and (3) he must **build** and **plant**, which means he must preach about hope and renewal."[xxi]

All prophets do not have the same anointing or spiritual assignments. Some are called to prophesy to the people, some to persons in government, some to individuals, and some to geographic regions, mountains, land, rivers, etc. In addition, some receive prophecies more frequently than others. "Do not despise prophecies, but test everything; hold fast what is good."[xxii]

We are not to blindly accept what is prophesied. In church, "[l]et two or three prophets speak and let the others weigh what is said. If a revelation is made to another sitting there, let the first be silent. For you can all prophesy one by one, so that all may learn and all be encouraged, and the spirits of prophets are subject to prophets."[xxiii] A prophet may be male or female.[xxiv]

My personal prayer is that you will be enlightened, strengthened, and encouraged as you study this workbook and record what God, Jesus, and The Holy Spirit reveal to you. Time spent with Them along with reading and studying the Bible yields great dividends.

Please check out my new website: **www.sheilaeismann.com**

Also, if you would like to send an email or have questions about this workbook, my address is **sheila@sheilaeismann.com**. Thank you!

"The LORD bless you and keep you;
 The LORD make His face shine upon you,
And be gracious to you;
The LORD lift up His countenance upon you,
And give you peace." (Numbers 6:24-26)

Our Sphere Of Authority

May 24, 2021
Prophetic Words

During the past few days, The Holy Spirit has been impressing upon me the importance of staying within our sphere of authority and making certain of our spiritual assignments. This is especially important in light of the days in which we are living with ongoing, tumultuous activity throughout the earth.

Since I'm also a western fiction author as well as a prophetic blogger, the accompanying image The Holy Spirit gave me corresponding to this timely reminder was that of a cowboy lassoing a steer inside a rodeo arena.

Oftentimes our brothers and sisters in Christ will try to "lasso" us into their specific spiritual assignments. While this can and does apply at certain times to complete corporate spiritual projects, we must still carefully discern whether or not we have permission to participate.

The life of the Apostle Paul in the New Testament is very instructive on so many levels. Even though he lived in the first century, it's as if time has stood still with respect to his spiritual applications and lessons.

False apostles continually rose up against Paul, a true apostle and one who was appointed by Jesus Christ. (Romans 1:1and Galatians 1:1)

The pertinent Biblical text for this week's blog post can be found in 2 Corinthians 10:7-18.

The Reality of The Apostle Paul's Authority

"Do you look at things according to the outward appearance? If anyone is convinced in himself that he is Christ's, let him again consider this in himself, that just as he *is* Christ's, even so we *are* Christ's. For even if I should boast somewhat more about our authority, which the Lord gave us for edification and not for your destruction, I shall not be ashamed— lest I seem to terrify you by letters. 'For *his* letters,' they say, '*are* weighty and powerful, but *his* bodily presence *is* weak, and *his* speech contemptible.' Let such a person consider this, that what we are in word by letters when we are absent, such *we will* also *be* in deed when we are present." (2 Corinthians 10:7-11)

The Limits of The Apostle Paul's Authority

"For we dare not class ourselves or compare ourselves with those who commend themselves. But they, measuring themselves by themselves, and comparing themselves among themselves, are not wise. We, however, will not boast beyond measure, but within the limits of the sphere which God appointed us—a sphere which especially includes you. For we are not overextending ourselves (as though *our authority* did not extend to you), for it was to you that we came with the gospel of Christ; not boasting of things beyond measure, *that is,* in other men's labors, but having hope, *that* as your faith is increased, we shall be greatly enlarged by you in our sphere, to preach the gospel in the *regions* beyond you, *and* not to boast in another man's sphere of accomplishment. (2 Corinthians 10:12-16)

"But '*he who glories, let him glory in the Lord.*' For not he who commends himself is approved, but whom the Lord commends." (2 Corinthians 10:17-18)

Lessons From Paul's Sphere of Authority

#1. The Lord Jesus gave it to him for his (Paul's) edification.

#2. It's not given for destruction.

#3. There's no shame in it.

#4. Paul is confident and gently reminds the church at Corinth of his assurance in Christ and challenges them regarding their attitudes.

#5. Humility is one of wisdom's sisters. Paul's maturity in Christ caused him to realize the danger of classing himself or comparing himself to those who commend themselves. Pride has many snares and traps inherent within it.

#6. One of the major successes of the Apostle Paul's ministry was that he recognized his sphere of authority and did not operate or venture beyond it.

Testimony Regarding Violating The Sphere Of Authority Principle

There can be a terrible price to pay if we don't stay within the sphere of authority allotted to us.

In 2003, I met a regional prophetess from our area who informed me that a horrific thing happened to five women who attended the same church she did. Since we live in a mountainous area, these 5 women had formed a prayer group and decided they were going to take on the principalities and powers present during that time frame. Tragically, all 5 of these women died of the same type of rare cancer.

I most certainly am not making light of the horrible misfortune experienced by these five Christian women, and perhaps there was no direct connection between their choice to go head-to-head with these principalities; however, when the prophetess told me this, I heeded the warning and found it to be most instructive.

We cannot conduct spiritual warfare in the flesh. (2 Corinthians 10:4-6)

When we step out of our assigned sphere of authority, we may not be under God's protection.

Prophetic Insights For Daily Living

#1. Just like the Apostle Paul, there is a **reality** to our sphere of authority and a **limit** to our sphere of authority. The same is true of any Christian irrespective of their gifting or calling. Paul was the apostle called to the Gentiles, and Peter was the apostle called to the Jews. (Galatians 2:8-9)
#2. Seek God with all of your heart, and He will outline and direct this for you by and through The Holy Spirit.
#3. What has God called/assigned you to do in His Kingdom?

_____
_____
_____
_____

#4. You will have a supernatural peace while doing what God has assigned you to do even if there are challenges along the way.

#5. Your work will bear fruit. The life of the Apostle Paul reflects this.

#6. You will have a zeal and passion for what you are called to do.

#7. The Holy Spirit may forbid you to do things to keep you within your assigned sphere of authority. Paul was forbidden to go to Asia during a specific time frame.

"Now when they had gone through Phrygia and the region of Galatia, they were forbidden by the Holy Spirit to preach the word in Asia. After they had come to Mysia, they tried to go into Bithynia, but the Spirit did not permit them. So passing by Mysia, they came down to Troas. And a vision appeared to Paul in the night. A man of Macedonia stood and pleaded with him, saying, 'Come over to Macedonia and help us.' Now after he had seen the vision, immediately we sought to go to Macedonia, concluding that the Lord had called us to preach the gospel to them." (Acts 16:6-10)

Paul went up to the church at Galatia by revelation. (Galatians 1:1 and Acts 16:9-10) The Holy Spirit will provide revelation to you as to where you are to go and what you are to do when you get there.

Ask for Godly wisdom, and God will give it to you. James 3:13-18. You can check this out for characteristics of Godly wisdom if you so desire:

https://www.kathyhoward.org/8-characteristics-of-wisdom/
https://sheilaeismann.com/heart-of-wisdom/

Some of your fellow Christians may become upset with you but make sure to extend grace and forgiveness to them as you explain your specific sphere of authority and the importance of staying and operating within it.

Whether you enjoy the western lifestyle with rodeos, cattle, horses, etc., or whatever your personal preference, keep an eye out for the "lasso" effect.

As we say in the west, "Cowboy up" or "Cowgirl up" which will help you to stay within your sphere of authority.

God bless, take care, and have a fruit-bearing week in our Lord and Savior, Jesus Christ.

Sheila Eismann, Prophetic Seer, Blogger, Author & Teacher, publishes her weekly blog posts endeavoring to encourage others through God's word. Her writings include teaching and instructions on how to apply prophetic insights for daily living. Please subscribe to receive new blog posts on her website at www.sheilaeismann.com. by clicking the "Subscribe" button in the far upper right-hand corner of her Home webpage.

Sheila Eismann

Growing In Hope – Petal # 1

June 1, 2021
Prophetic Teachings

As spring transitions into summer, my spirit has been stirred by a recent prophetic picture I've been given. It's a beautiful flower with 8 elongated petals. The center is bright red bearing the name of **_Jesus_** Who holds all things together including every flower that is created. Supernaturally brushed across each petal is an aspect of hope to cause us to grow in Jesus Christ, our precious Lord and Savior. Suffice it to say, there are many facets and characteristics to hope itself.

Over the next few weeks, I'll be touching upon the ones revealed to me in this prophetic vision as I launch this Growing in Hope series. This one challenges us to look for the good in all things.

According to Colossians 1:17, "He (Jesus) is before all things, and in him all things hold together." (NIV) This is why His name is located in the center of this eternal flower with its 8 everlasting petals. Flowers are symbolic of the righteous, prosperity, brevity of life, offering of praise (fragrance) to Christ, clothing, life, and glory.

Proverbs 13:12 states, "Hope deferred makes the heart sick,
But *when* the desire comes, *it is* a tree of life."

What if the thing or outcome you've hoped for never arrives or materializes?

It can lead to situations, feelings, and attitudes far beyond just being heartsick not to mention never growing into a tree of life.

Introspection, Contemplation, and Reflection

The tenor of this week's blog post and the subsequent ones to follow are tailored toward introspection, contemplation, and reflection. Allow them to marinate in your soul, mind, and spirit toward the end goal of growing in hope.

I've not spoken with anyone or read of a single account of late wherein there's not been at least a twinge of lost hope as it's crashed on the rocks of reality.

Some of these cases are of our own making whereas others are completely out of our control. It's at this intersection of life that we have a choice to make. We can either start to spiral downward or grab onto Jesus, the author, and finisher of our faith. Our hope in Him is the anchor of our soul (Hebrews 6:19)

Petal # 1 – Romans 8:28

Much to my surprise, Petal #1 emerged bearing Romans 8:28.

When writing to the church in Rome, the Apostle Paul drilled down on the bandwidth of suffering to eternal glory in a stretch of narrow verses penned in Romans 8:18-30.

Romans 8:28 reads,

"And we know that **all things** work together for **good** to those who love God, to those who are the called according to *His* purpose." (Emphasis mine) The Greek word for good in this verse is *agathos* which means:

#1. of good constitution or nature

#2. useful, salutary

#3. good, pleasant, agreeable, joyful, happy

#4. excellent, distinguished

#5. upright, honourable

https://www.blueletterbible.org/lang/Lexicon/Lexicon.cfm?strongs=G18&t=KJV

It's flat out amazing that the Apostle Paul maintained the attitude that he did and maintained a proper spiritual perspective in light of all that he experienced after his dramatic conversion on the road to Damascus. (Read Acts Chapter 9)

https://sheilaeismann.com/clear-vision/

Paul was rejected, betrayed, beaten, falsely accused, stoned, shipwrecked, in many perils of various kinds, hungry, thirsty, and weary beyond measure. (2 Corinthians 11:22-29)

Before his conversion, Paul was married. (1 Corinthians 7:8-9) In the Bible, he does not indicate if his wife passed away or if he was divorced. (1 Corinthians 7:8-9; 9:5)) https://churchleaders.com/outreach-missions/outreach-missions-articles/321152-was-the-apostle-paul-married-yes-he-was-heres-how-we-know-denny-burke.html

For me personally, the loss of a loved one challenges Romans 8:28 to its very core even after going through all of the horrible stages of grief.

As contrary as it might seem, it's the very word **good** in Romans 8:28 that is going to help continue to propel us forward in the days ahead. We must search for it like the zealous gold or silver miner searches intently for his treasure. A loss would be included in the "all things" in this verse. Even though it may take time, we must make an intentional choice to look for the good.

King David, no stranger to loss and hardship, encourages us in Psalm 16:9b, "My flesh also will rest in hope." This is a tall order since it's our flesh that tends to scream the loudest!

We've just celebrated Memorial Day in our nation including paying honor and tribute to those who gave their lives for freedom. My father was a World War II Veteran, and my husband is a Viet Nam Veteran. I will be forever grateful to them and the countless others who answered the call of duty.

Prophetic Insights For Daily Living:

One of my "Sheilaisms" is, "Teamwork makes it happen!" To that end, I would invite you to reply to my blog post to help all of us as we continue growing in hope.

#1. What depletes your hope, and how have you gained the victory over this?
_____
_____
_____

#2. What dashes your hope, and how have you rebuilt it?
_____
_____
_____

#3. What has helped restore your hope?
_____
_____
_____

#4. How have you ultimately found the **_good_** in Romans 8:28?
_____
_____
_____

#5. What is your #1 hope today?
_____

I would encourage you to record it. After we've touched the 8 petals of the eternal flower, double back here to see how you're growing in hope.

Since we can't control everything or everyone in our lives, HOPE is the daily spiritual infusion that keeps us going.

I would like to share a little of my free-flowing acrostic poetry with you. God sends His hope to:

H – Help
O – Overcome
P – Problems
E – Everyday

While reading this blog, may you be reminded that our awesome God, His Son, Jesus Christ, and The Holy Spirit have given you a fresh start, **_a new hope_**, and a heart filled with abundant reasons to be thankful and joyful as you continue to look for the good in all things.

Sheila Eismann, Prophetic Seer, Blogger, Author & Teacher, publishes her weekly blog posts endeavoring to encourage others through God's word. Her writings include teaching and instructions on how to apply prophetic insights for daily living. Please subscribe to receive new blog posts on her website at www.sheilaeismann.com. by clicking the "Subscribe" button in the far upper right-hand corner of her Home webpage.

Growing In Hope – Petal # 2

June 8, 2021
Prophetic Teachings

As we continue with our growing in hope series, Petal #2 manifested in the heavenly vision from The Holy Spirit as "Abide in Christ." Any temporal hopes the world might have to offer vanish day by day, but we have the eternal hope in Jesus Christ our Lord when we accept Him as our personal Lord and Savior and continue to walk with and serve Him. (Titus 1:2 and 3:6-7) Abiding is the key.

Quite possibly the best lifelong example of someone in the Old Testament regarding the subject of abiding is the prophet, Samuel. When he was weaned, his mother, Hannah, took him to the house of the Lord in Shiloh.

"Now the man Elkanah (Hannah's husband) and all his house went up to offer to the Lord the yearly sacrifice and his vow. But Hannah did not go up, for she said to her husband, '*Not* until the child is weaned; then I will take him, that he may appear before the Lord and remain there forever.'" (1 Samuel 1:21-22)

One important takeaway from Hannah's life is that she abided in God before He gave her Samuel, despite all those challenges, and continued to do so afterward.

Samuel did serve as prophet, judge, and priest. He was the last judge of Israel and the first prophet following Moses. He followed Eli as the high priest for the nation of Israel. We learn from this Biblical example the importance of generational abiding.

Can you think of families who have benefited from the blessing of generational abiding or is yours one of them? If not, it's never too late to start!

_____

_____

Fast forward to those of us living under the New Covenant today, and even if we weren't dedicated as a young child to the Lord or grew up in a Christian home, we can still abide with Jesus Christ forever. Eternity is a very long time. We may not be a prophet or judge like Samuel was, but we are kings and priests according to 1 Peter 2:9 and Revelation 5:10.

Suffice it to say, there's a physical place to abide and a spiritual place to abide. (Proverbs 7:11; Luke 24:29) Your address may be 1234 Easy Street, Wonderful World, USA 11111, but where are you abiding spiritually?

https://sheilaeismann.com/look-for-the-good/

Perhaps your mind and spirit have already jumped ahead to the 15th chapter of the gospel of John which addresses, the true vine (Jesus), the vinedresser, (God, the Father), and the branches (Christian believers in Jesus).
John 15:1-8 states,

"I am the true vine, and My Father is the vinedresser. Every branch in Me that does not bear fruit He takes away; and every *branch* that bears fruit He prunes, that it may bear more fruit. You are already clean because of the word which I have spoken to you. Abide in Me, and I in you. As the branch cannot bear fruit of itself, unless it abides in the vine, neither can you, unless you abide in Me.

"I am the vine, you *are* the branches. He who abides in Me, and I in him, bears much fruit; for without Me you can do nothing. If anyone does not abide in Me, he is cast out as a branch and is withered; and they gather them and throw *them* into the fire, and they are burned. If you abide in Me, and My words abide in you, you will ask what you desire, and it shall be done for you. By this My Father is glorified, that you bear much fruit; so you will be My disciples."

The Greek word for abide in the above verses is the verb *meno* (Strong's G3306) which has the following meanings:

I. To remain, abide
   A. In reference to place
      i. To sojourn, tarry
      ii. Not to depart
         a. To continue to be present
         b. To be held, kept, continually
   B. In reference to time
      i. To continue to be, not to perish, to last, endure
         a. Of persons, to survive, live
   C. In reference to state or condition
      i. To remain as one, not to become another or different
II. To wait for, await one

https://www.blueletterbible.org/lexicon/g3306/kjv/tr/0-1/

When reading over the above list, the one definition which resonated with me was B in reference to time, and in particular, subsection i. which reads, "To continue to be, not to perish, to last, endure."

Also, to remain in or with someone, we must remain united with the person in one heart, mind, and will. The opposite would also be true, i.e., to abide with someone and not be united to him. If we continually abide in Christ, we will not perish, but we will endure in Him.

As you read and ponder John 15 and the definitions of the Greek word *meno*, what revelatory downloads, quickenings, challenges, encouragement, etc. are you receiving? I would encourage you to record them here, so when we are complete with this series, you can reflect upon what God has been showing you in real-time as true Christianity is never stagnant as we continue with our journey and process of sanctification.

_____
_____
_____
_____
_____
_____
_____
_____
_____

Follow the Apostle Paul as he follows Christ:

If you would like to discover one of the keys to how the Apostle Paul gained hope and maintained confidence in his ministry, please read the entire chapter of 2 Corinthians 3. What keen insight can you glean from this?

_____
_____
_____
_____

Let patience have its perfect work:

I'd be amazed at the number of people who would even entertain the thought of including the word **patient** in their all-time 10 favorite vocabulary words; however, life requires it on many levels. Put the heavy scope on these verses:

Romans 15:4

1 Thessalonians 1:2-4

1 Timothy 6:11

James 1:2-4

How do you think patience and hope work hand in hand?

_____
_____

Prophetic Insights For Daily Living:

#1. What's gnawing at you to prevent you from 100% abiding in Christ, if anything at all? If you're already there, I rejoice with you. Hallelujah!

_____
_____

#2. We will receive a reward for abiding in Christ. (1 Corinthians 3:14)

#3. While we abide in Christ, we continue to be taught by The Holy Spirit. (1 John 2:24-27)

#4. Abiding is the key. If we choose to continue to abide in Christ, we may have confidence in Him and not be ashamed at His coming. We will not face the condemnation of the Great White Throne Judgment as our names are written in the Lamb's Book of Life. (1 John 2:28; Revelation 20:11-15)

#5. Psalm 91 is a wonderful and comforting passage of scripture to read daily as you choose to abide in Jesus. What additional Bible verses would you suggest to others?

_____
_____

I'll close this week's blog post with Jesus' words from John 15:9-11,

"As the Father loved Me, I have loved you; abide in My love. If you keep My commandments, you will abide in My love, just as I have kept My Father's commandments and abide in His love."

Sheila Eismann, Prophetic Seer, Blogger, Author & Teacher, publishes her weekly blog posts endeavoring to encourage others through God's word. Her writings include teaching and instructions on how to apply prophetic insights for daily living.

Please subscribe to receive new blog posts on her website at www.sheilaeismann.com. by clicking the "Subscribe" button in the far upper right-hand corner of her Home webpage.

Sheila Eismann

Growing in Hope – Petal # 3

June 14, 2021
Prophetic Teachings

#Gratitudeisanattitude may be a worn-out hashtag, but there's definitely spiritual merit within it. Petal # 3 of my *Growing in Hope* series is thankfulness or expressing gratitude to God no matter what is going on in our lives. He is looking for grateful hearts.

A Living Hope Tied To A Heavenly Inheritance

While the beautiful, yellow flower with 8 elongated petals and the bright red center bearing the name of **Jesus** is not a living flower, the hope expressed therein is a living hope in our Lord and Savior, Jesus Christ.

"Blessed *be* the God and Father of our Lord Jesus Christ, who according to His abundant mercy has begotten us again to a living hope through the resurrection of Jesus Christ from the dead, to an inheritance incorruptible and undefiled and that does not fade away, reserved in heaven for you, who are kept by the power of God through faith for salvation ready to be revealed in the last time." (1 Peter 1:3-5)

Some of us may not receive inheritances of land, ranches, buildings, businesses, money, vehicles, coin collections, art work, or you fill in the blank _____
_____.

If we are believers in Jesus Christ, we are guaranteed to receive the most important inheritance, which is incorruptible and will never fade away.

We won't be able to take our earthly inheritances to heaven with us. (Job 1:21 and Ecclesiastes 5:15) There used to be an old joke something along the lines that no one ever saw a man with a fleet of trailers hauling his stuff to heaven after he died. Our angels have their assignments, but this is not one of them. (Matthew 18:10 and Acts 12:15)

The Heart Soil Of Gratitude

During times of loss, disappointment, betrayal, crisis, etc., the soil of our hearts can become as hard as concrete if we allow it to do so. Destructive seeds cannot grow in the heart soil of thankfulness and gratitude.

The person who embraces and expresses gratitude is beyond thankful for what they do have and is not constantly seeking more. Life does not consist of an abundance of things. (Luke 12:15) A person can possess every earthly thing possible and still have a bankrupt soul, unfortunately.

When I consulted the dictionary definition of the word gratitude, I was struck by the portion of the meaning which read, "readiness to show appreciation for and to return kindness."

In addition to "the quality of being thankful," we could add the choice to be thankful. Choosing to be thankful is a choice just like anything else in life.

grat·i·tude

noun

1. the quality of being thankful; readiness to show appreciation for and to return kindness.

https://www.google.com/search?q=definition+of+gratitude&rlz=1C1CHBF_enUS800US801&oq=definition+of+gratitude&aqs=chrome..69i57j0l6j0i22i30l3.5321j1j7&sourceid=chrome&ie=UTF-8

A truly thankful person doesn't just wait for the national holiday of Thanksgiving to express gratitude. It's in operation 24-7/365 days a year.

https://sheilaeismann.com/give-thanks-in-everything/

Biblical Examples of Gratitude

What's your favorite passage of the Bible addressing the subject of gratitude or thankfulness?

_____
_____
_____

One of mine is the account of King David and Abigail, the original wife of Nabal and ultimate bride of the king.

Years ago, I was asked to speak at a Christian Women's gathering at the Nazareth Retreat Center in our valley. Each presenter was assigned the general topic of wisdom. I was drawn to the life of Abigail as I deem her a very wise woman.

I can only imagine that at the time Abigail was loading the bread, dressed sheep, cakes, and figs onto donkeys that she never dreamed it would end up with a marriage proposal. (1 Samuel 25:39)

Trust me, I would never make it as the third of any man's eight simultaneous wives; however, we know from Biblical history this was part of Abigail's destiny. Why do you think she was willing to leave all of the luxuries and trappings of the Carmel Estate for a man who had been living in caves and strongholds and did not have enough to eat most of the time? (1 Samuel 22:1-2)

_____
_____
_____

Abigail was put in a situation or circumstance that was out of her control because of her derelict husband, Nabal, whose name means "fool." (1 Samuel 25:25) When she was put to the test, she passed it with flying colors because she was a woman of substance who was filled with the fear of the Lord and much Godly wisdom, and she operated from a grateful heart. She exercised her gratitude swiftly and mightily, and the rest is Biblical history!

Prophetic Insights for Daily Living

#1. Why and how do you think gratitude is tied to kindness?
_____
_____
_____

#2. Has anyone ever done anything kind or unexpected for you when you were really down and out or suffering horribly? _____
    If so, how did this make you feel?
_____
_____

    Did it infuse hope within you? _____

    Conversely, have you taken action to help someone during their hour of trial? _____

    If so, how did this make you feel?
_____

    Did it infuse hope within you? _____

    Even if the person never thanked you or showed any appreciation for your act of kindness, did you continue to extend grace to him or her and not allow a seed of bitterness to take root in your heart?
_____

Practical Steps & A Call To Action

Years ago, there was a popular acronym developed for prayer which was:

A – Adoration
C – Confession
T – Thanksgiving

S – Supplication

From the above list, these were the four steps encouraging Christians to use when praying to God. Perhaps some of you still implement this practice. The order is quite straightforward, but more importantly, thanksgiving or gratitude is not omitted.

Imagine if you are the type of person who walks in gratitude and thanksgiving every single day and lives next door to a crabby neighbor. For ten years straight hand running, you went out of your way to help Mr. or Mrs. Crabby who never thanked you once. Can you see a heavenly picture in all of this?

Since God will not override man's free will, horrible things happen in our world every day; however, there's still the choice to trust God in all things and continue to express our gratitude to Him. Perhaps some days are so bleak all we can thank Him for is a sunrise, sunset, the song of a bird as we walk down the street, or a stranger's smile.

May we continue to look and listen for even the smallest of things for which to be grateful and express our thanksgiving on earth to whom it's due, but ultimately to our Heavenly Father, Who is always on the lookout for grateful hearts.

Fellow saints and believers, may we be eternally grateful to God, Jesus, and The Holy Spirit and for Their manifest presence in our lives. They are for us, love us, and are working on our behalf even if we don't readily discern it.

"Enter into His gates with thanksgiving,
And into His courts with praise.
Be thankful to Him, and bless His name." (Psalm 100:4)

Sheila Eismann, Prophetic Seer, Blogger, Author & Teacher, publishes her weekly blog posts endeavoring to encourage others through God's word. Her writings include teaching and instructions on how to apply prophetic insights for daily living.

Please subscribe to receive new blog posts on her website at www.sheilaeismann.com. by clicking the "Subscribe" button in the far upper right-hand corner of her Home webpage.

Growing in Hope – Petal # 4

June 22, 2021
Prophetic Teachings

On a scale of 1-10, what's your patience level these days? In the wild western part of the United States, we're experiencing an early, unprecedented heatwave that tends to tax even the most patient of sweet souls. We're living in a bake oven every single day with not a drop of rain on the horizon. For those of you following and reading my weekly blog posts, I'm confident that some of you just knew one of the petals of the yellow, supernatural flower of hope was eventually going to be patience.

This week's blog post is specially designed with many reflective aspects, questions, and contemplations. Also, I've included an invitation to share your spiritual growth comments with others.

When we became Christians, my husband and I started attending a local, evening Bible Study at the home of a mature Christian couple who ultimately ended up becoming our spiritual parents. We'd only been there a couple of months when Jim, the group discussion leader, decided we would study the book of James. Keep in mind that at this juncture of my life, I had virtually no authentic Christian background or solid Biblical foundation.

Even though there are only 5 chapters to the book of James, it packs a bold, spiritual punch. It's not for the faint of heart, but then again, it was written in approximately AD 45 by Jesus's half-brother to the 12 tribes which were scattered abroad. After the dispersion of the early church, new Christians were definitely experiencing trials and hardships.

It could well be that James penned this letter via the inspiration of The Holy Spirit because while Jesus walked the earth, James himself was not a

Christian. He did not follow his half-brother during this time. (Mark 3:21-35). It was after witnessing Jesus's resurrection that James became one of the pillars of the early church. (1 Corinthians 15:7 and Galatians 2:9) God was certainly patient with him just like He is with each of us. Aren't you thankful for God's patience and longsuffering?

In retrospect, can you see how God used James' impatience ultimately for good for the whole world? Each time we read the book he authored with The Holy Spirit's help, we can offer a prayer of thanksgiving.

Jim, Our Bible Study Discussion Leader

Back to Jim, our Bible Study discussion leader, for a moment. I can still hear his voice 38 years later when he started to read the first chapter of James. My spirit stopped on these three verses:

"My brethren, count it all joy when you fall into various trials, knowing that the testing of your faith produces patience. But let patience have *its* perfect work, that you may be perfect and complete, lacking nothing." (James 1:2-4)

Perfect in the above verse is Strong's G5046 which is the Greek word ***teleios*** and means brought to its end, finished; lacking nothing necessary to completeness; perfect.

https://www.blueletterbible.org/lexicon/g5046/kjv/tr/0-1/

It's important to keep in mind that we're not expected to be perfect as there's only been one perfect human being, and that is Jesus Christ, the Son of God. Obviously, the emphasis is upon lacking nothing necessary to complete whatever is needed in our lives or the situation at hand.

Little did I know that within 3 short months of starting our study in James, my husband would lose his job due to no fault of his own as a result of him taking a stand for justice and righteousness. We had no money in the bank and did not know where our next paycheck was coming from. This was during a harsh winter in our desert valley with 3-4 feet of standing snow. We drove an old, temperamental diesel car at that time which really did not like cold weather. There was no money for Christmas gifts. We had empty briefcases and the shirts on our backs.

But we also had God, Jesus, The Holy Spirit, God's angels, God's word, and our Bible Study group on our side. Suffice it to say, this was **<u>not</u>** the introduction to Christianity that I expected nor was I counting it all joy while God was building patience and hope within us.
Can you think of a time in your life when something adverse and unexpected happened? What was the ultimate outcome, and what did the testing of your faith produce?

Patience – A Supernatural Boundary Line

Patience is sort of like a supernatural boundary line in our lives that keeps us in line with hope. If we stray outside the boundary lines, we lose patience which causes us to lose hope. What happens to us when we lose hope?

Applying the Scriptures to Your Situation

What Biblical scriptures have ministered to you when you've been challenged with impatience or a lack of hope?

I welcome you to leave a comment at the end of this blog post to share with others who may benefit from your spiritual growth.

Prophetic Insights for Daily Living

#1. We must possess patience to have hope.
#2. What impatience do you need to give to God or ask Him to remove from you?
_____
_____
_____

#3. What causes you to become impatient?
_____
_____
_____

#4. What do you need to do to grow in patience, and why do we even need it?
_____
_____
_____

#5. Patience is listed a fruit of the Spirit outlined in Galatians 5:22-23. (NIV)
#6. Why is it so hard to exercise patience during our trials and tribulations?
_____

#7. Have you ever prayed for patience?

#8. Has there been a time when your impatience developed into patience in a profitable manner? If so, what was it?

#9. Other than patience, can you deem what else God is building and shaping within you when you've gone through a difficult journey?

#10. If you do not become easily irritated at trying situations or circumstances, pray for those who do.

<u>The Maturity Is In The Waiting</u>

Here's a blog post I've previously written that you may enjoy reading as a companion to the one this week.

https://sheilaeismann.com/freedom-from-anxiety/

"Therefore be patient, brethren, until the coming of the Lord. See *how* the farmer waits for the precious fruit of the earth, waiting patiently for it until it receives the early and latter rain. You also be patient. Establish your hearts, for the coming of the Lord is at hand. (James 5:7-8)

Patience can be required for a short period of time or a lengthy one.

In Luke 21:19, Jesus instructed His disciples, "By your patience possess your souls." Since we are His disciples, how does this apply to us today and in the future?

We are to take our hope and share it with others. Now that we're halfway through the 8 petals on the supernatural hope flower, how are some of the ways that you've been able to do this?

"Now may the God of hope fill you with all joy and peace in believing, that you may abound in hope by the power of the Holy Spirit." (Romans 15:13)

Sheila Eismann, Prophetic Seer, Blogger, Author & Teacher, publishes her weekly blog posts endeavoring to encourage others through God's word. Her writings include teaching and instructions on how to apply prophetic insights for daily living.

Please subscribe to receive new blog posts on her website at www.sheilaeismann.com. by clicking the "Subscribe" button in the far upper right-hand corner of her Home webpage.

The New, Big Bend In The River Of Your Life

June 28, 2021
Prophetic Teachings

Instead of continuing with the *Growing in Hope* series that I've been posting on my website for the past month, it's time to hit the pause button to share a recent, encouraging vision with you. So, I'm implementing some lingo from the old tv commercials which went something along the lines of, "I'll be right back after this important message." Ergo, Petal # 5 on the supernatural hope flower will appear next week. It's time for us to focus upon the new, big bend in the river of your life which highlights millennials.

Last week as we were leading up to our awesome family reunion which included several millennials, the Spirit realm opened, and I saw the following:

There was a big, wide bend in the river to the right which looked like a tree trunk. The water was solid green instead of the traditional blue and showed no signs of algae, weeds, or concerning issues.

A river is symbolic of The Holy Spirit, a move of the Spirit, the word of God, and the river of life. I knew by revelation that this new bend and river flow pertained to the river of life. There was a large volume of water being released into this new direction.

It's sort of a play on words using the term *right* which symbolizes correctness, authority, longevity, wisdom, and strength (think of God's righteous right hand as mentioned in Isaiah 41:10). The right hand denotes the mouth whereas the left one is the heart.

In addition, with the water being a healthy green, this represents new growth, something new in your life, prosperity, life, increase, bearing fruit, the anointing (olive green), and joy. Granted, there are negative aspects to the color green, but since the condition of the water was healthy, I'm focusing upon the positive side of my favorite color.

The Fish Are Hungry

Three more days went by, and scene # 2 of the vision unfolded showing innumerable fish jumping high above the water. They were very hungry and were snatching and gulping down the insects flying above their heads.

Just for grins, you might want to check out this website article regarding the 7 reasons fish jump out of the water.

https://www.slo-fishing.si/fishing-for-beginners/315-why-do-fish-jump-out-of-the-water

I will be focusing upon Reason # 2 which is to get food. Some of the remaining 6 reasons might surprise you a little bit as well.

Fish symbolize the souls of men, believers in Christ, potential believers in Jesus, the gospel – spiritual food, or revival. The fish in the big bend in the river were smaller fish which I deem represent younger people but especially the Millennials as they are affectionately referred to these days.

The Valley of Decision

In the Old Testament, the prophet Joel referred to multitudes being in the valley of decision.

Joel 3:14 states, "Multitudes, multitudes in the valley of decision! For the day of the Lord *is* near in the valley of decision."

The valley of decision is also the Valley of King Jehoshaphat which means "Yahweh judges." The geographical location is most likely the Kidron Valley which is on the east side of Jerusalem.

The Biblical context of Joel 3 is the time when God will judge the earth and render His decision at the end of the tribulation period referenced in Daniel 9:24-27 coupled with Matthew 24:15 and 25:31-46, Revelation 11:2-3, Revelation chapter 13 and 14:14-20.

Immediately following the fulfillment of this prophecy of judgment will be the advent of Jesus' Millennial reign which is a literal 1,000 time period wherein He will rule as King from Jerusalem. (Daniel 7:11-13 and Revelation 20:1-7)

There's an intriguing inference in this prophetic vision. Now is the time to reach out to the Millennial generation born between 1980 and 2000. They are also known as Generation Y or the Net Generation. That's fascinating because sometimes you need a net to fully secure a fish that you've caught using a fishing pole since fish symbolize the souls of people. If you are a Millennial who's reading this blog post, please reach out to a fellow Millennial.

The fish jumping out of the water are trying to get spiritual food. This doesn't just pertain to the younger people. People all over the world are physically and spiritually hungry right now, especially following a global pandemic in which many perished, unfortunately.

On The River Banks

In the last scene of this prophetic vision, I saw people standing on both sides of the river. They were clapping, smiling, jumping up and down, singing, and shouting. Not only were the fish jumping, but humanity was jumping right along with them!

Standing in this large crowd, I specifically saw three people who accepted Jesus Christ as their personal Lord and Savior before they died:

#1. My brother, Jeff

#2. My father

#3. My mother

The reason I've listed them in this order is because that's the timeframe in which they graduated to heaven. My brother attended college in the south and lived there as an adult with his family. He loved the water, swimming, diving, and going on cruises. I know these specific family members to be a portion of the cloud of witnesses in heaven who are cheering all of us on to complete our race and win the prize.

Hebrews 12:1-2, "Therefore we also, since we are surrounded by so great a cloud of witnesses, let us lay aside every weight, and the sin which so easily ensnares *us*, and let us run with endurance the race that is set before us, looking unto Jesus, the author and finisher of *our* faith, who for the joy that was set before Him endured the cross, despising the shame, and has sat down at the right hand of the throne of God."

2 Timothy 4:7, "I have fought the good fight, I have finished the race, I have kept the faith."

A Word in Due Season

I deem this is a "now word" or a "word in due season."

"A man has joy by the answer of his mouth,
And a word *spoken* in due season, how good *it is!*" (Proverbs 15:23)
Earlier in this blog post, I mentioned that one of the symbolisms for right is the right hand which is the mouth.

For an additional resource, during 2020 I authored a blog titled "The Frozen Footprint" which is helpful for the context of this prophetic vision. Here's the link: https://sheilaeismann.com/seek-the-lost/

Prophetic Insights For Daily Living

#1. In which direction is the river of your life currently flowing?

#2. Do you sense it's going in the right way to fulfill the call of God upon your life?

#3. Are you ready to go with the new, big bend in the river of your life?

#4. Who's included in the cloud of witnesses in your family or your life?

#5. What's your attitude toward the Millennial Generation or are you a Millennial? If so, what helpful suggestions could you offer?

A Call To Action

Since this river is a living, giving, and sustaining one, it could be life-changing for some of you. If you have been writing in your prophetic journal as I've previously recommended, this would be an important entry with details as they unfold over the summer months.

Revisit the prophetic symbolism for the various aspects of this prophetic vision to see if any of them resonate with your spirit such as something new in your life as evidenced by the green-colored water in the new, big bend in the river of your life.

You can yield to the supernatural bend in the river of your life or continue in the direction you're heading now.

Lavish love upon a Millennial or whomever The Holy Spirit is highlighting in your life this summer because genuine love changes everything.

Sheila Eismann, Prophetic Seer, Blogger, Author & Teacher, publishes her weekly blog posts endeavoring to encourage others through God's word. Her writings include teaching and instructions on how to apply prophetic insights for daily living.

Please subscribe to receive new blog posts on her website at www.sheilaeismann.com. by clicking the "Subscribe" button in the far upper right-hand corner of her Home webpage.

Growing in Hope – Petal # 5

July 5, 2021
Prophetic Teachings

During the preparation time for this week's blog post, I was taken into the Spirit realm wherein I saw a woman who was trying to climb up the face of a sheer, granite rock wall using just a rope. Struggling to maintain her balance, she swayed back and forth as she desperately hung onto the rope with her feet dangling below her. This woman had no rock-climbing gear other than the rope. She'd neglected to take along the foundational elements for what she was attempting to do. While this may seem a strange introduction for the fifth petal in the eternal hope flower, it reinforces the importance to obey God and His word.

Just as there are essential pieces of gear for all outdoor rock climbs which you can check out via this weblink, https://sportrock.com/10-essential-pieces-of-gear-for-all-outdoor-climbs/, there are necessary pieces or elements to our Christian walk which will help us to obey God.

How is the command to obey God and His word linked to hope?

_____
_____

None of us is exempt from the storms of life. Hopefully, you're in a calm season right now, but sometimes, trials and tribulations seem to blow in when we least expect them. I deem the woman in the open vision is symbolic of anyone who's going through a supreme challenge of some sort right now.

Matthew 7:24-27 instructs us,

"Therefore whoever hears these sayings of Mine, and does them, I will liken him to a wise man who built his house on the rock: and the rain descended, the floods came, and the winds blew and beat on that house; and it did not fall, for it was founded on the rock.

"But everyone who hears these sayings of Mine, and does not do them, will be like a foolish man who built his house on the sand: and the rain descended, the floods came, and the winds blew and beat on that house; and it fell. And great was its fall."

In the above scriptures, Jesus spoke of two types of builders. Considering His description of them did He make it clear that they were judged:

(a) by the care and concern, they took in building their houses or
(b) by the foundation upon which they stood or
(c) both of the above?

_____
_____
_____

There's a companion portion of scripture in Luke 6:46-49 which reads,

"But why do you call Me 'Lord, Lord,' and not do the things which I say? Whoever **comes** to Me, and **hears** My sayings and **does** them, I will show you whom he is like: He is like a man building a house, who dug deep and laid the foundation on the rock. And when the flood arose, the stream beat vehemently against that house, and could not shake it, for it was founded on the rock. But he who heard and did nothing is like a man who built a house on the earth without a foundation, against which the stream beat vehemently; and immediately it fell. And the ruin of that house was great." (Emphases mine)

Inherent within the above-listed teaching are three requirements:

#1. Comes to Jesus which would include accepting Him as our personal Lord and Savior and making Him Lord of every area of our lives.
#2. Hears Jesus's sayings meaning reading and believing the Bible to be the inerrant word of God.
#3. Does them which means to obey God and His word.

A word of encouragement to a late or foolish builder.

As I've been praying into this prophetic teaching, the Lord is releasing encouragement to all of us from Lamentations 3:22-24,

"*Through* the LORD's mercies we are not consumed, Because His compassions fail not.
They are new every morning;
Great is Your faithfulness.

'The LORD is my portion,' says my soul,

'Therefore I **hope** in Him!'" (Emphasis mine)

God, Jesus, and The Holy Spirit desire to help us, especially in our time of greatest need. To obey God, we must have a repentant heart, and it's never too late to start. God's grace is always available to help us become a wise builder on the solid foundation of His Son, Jesus Christ of Nazareth, in Whom we have redemption from our sins and the hope of eternal life.

Outward obedience vs. inward obedience

Have you ever heard the saying, "Standing up on the outside but sitting down on the inside?"

This cliché has no age parameters. The Pharisees in the New Testament are a great example. When you read through the gospels, there are times when Jesus reads them the riot act for their behavior because they were doing the equivalent of standing up on the outside but sitting down on the inside. (Matthew 23:1-39 and Luke 11:37-54)

The main difference between the Pharisees and some of those around them in the gospel settings is that the Pharisees had the Torah but refused to obey God as it pertained to the acceptance of His Son, Jesus Christ, as the Messiah. In addition, they put more emphasis upon the traditions of men than the word of God. Isaiah 29:13 and Matthew 15:1-20 directly address this issue.

To obey God requires that we stand up both on the outside and the inside along with giving more credence to His word than the traditions of men.

The crux of obedience is a heart issue because it's with our hearts that we choose to obey. God is loving and gracious in this area as long as we are making a continued, positive effort.

Prophetic Insights For Daily Living

#1. In which area(s) of your life do you find it the most challenging to obey God and His word? Why is this, and what proactive steps can you take to overcome and gain the victory?

_____

_____

_____

#2. If we obey God as outlined in the Bible, we can show others the way to eternal life in Jesus and help them grow in hope.

#3. Earlier this year, I authored a blog post titled, "Beneficial Boundaries." Establishing healthy boundary lines and staying within them always help us to obey God.

https://sheilaeismann.com/broken-fence/

#4. Which trial, tribulation, disappointment, betrayal, disobedience or problem do you need to surrender to God to maintain your living hope in Him, the God of all hope?

_____
_____
_____

#5. Here are some suggested scriptures for you to study and meditate upon:

Psalm 119:47, 60

Psalm 128:1

Proverbs 4:20-21

John 14:23

Acts 5:32

James 1:22

1 John 2:17

"I wait for the Lord, my soul waits,
And in His word I do hope." (Psalm 130:5)

My sincere prayer is that as you're reading and studying these prophetic blog posts, hope is infused into your hearts, minds, souls, and spirits.

Have a blessed week in Jesus our Lord as we continue to live by faith, walk in love, extend forgiveness and grow in hope.

Sheila Eismann, Prophetic Seer, Blogger, Author & Teacher, publishes her weekly blog posts endeavoring to encourage others through God's word. Her writings include teaching and instructions on how to apply prophetic insights for daily living.

Please subscribe to receive new blog posts on her website at www.sheilaeismann.com. by clicking the "Subscribe" button in the far upper right-hand corner of her Home webpage.

Growing in Hope – Petal # 6

July 14, 2021
Prophetic Teachings

Joy, the 6th petal on the supernatural, yellow hope flower which manifested in the Spirit a few weeks ago, is a formidable weapon, a source of comfort and strength, and a very necessary part of our spiritual life. In Psalm 16, King David pours out his heart to God. Verse 11 gives us a major clue, "In Your presence *is* fullness of joy;" If our "joy tank" is running on empty or if we need more joy, we can follow the sage advice of Israel's beloved king and get into God's presence.

Getting Into God's Presence

What are some of the steps that you take to quiet your flesh in order to get into God's presence?

_____
_____
_____
_____

Here are some helpful suggestions if needed:

Step # 1. Praise – Envision Jesus stepping onto the balcony of His throne room in the third heaven and smiling as He hears our songs of praise! (Ezra 3:11; Psalms 7:17, 69:30, 95:1-3, 100:4-5 and 147:7; and Ephesians 5:18-20) Praise takes our minds off ourselves and directs our attention toward God. It releases whatever has our spirit bound such as tension, anger, unforgiveness, despair, sadness, grief, distraction, and hopelessness. The positive, spiritual exchange takes place as we continue to praise.

Step # 2. Prayer – Hebrews 4:16 assures us that we can come boldly to the throne of grace, that we may obtain mercy and find grace to help in time of need. God created us to communicate with Him, and the chief way we do this is through prayer. There can be times in life when we are so depleted, that it's extremely hard to pray. A suggestion would be to read the Psalms aloud which some consider being the equivalent of a type of prayer. (Also, Colossians 4:2 and 1 Thessalonians 5:16-18)

Step # 3. Read God's Word – "Be diligent to present yourself approved to God, a worker who does not need to be ashamed, rightly dividing the word of truth." (2 Timothy 2:15) Just as we need physical nourishment every day, our spirits require fortification from the Holy Bible which is the inerrant word of God.

Sometimes, as you read your Bible, The Holy Spirit will stop your spirit on a particular passage of scripture to render just exactly what you need. I've had this happen before, and the end result is amazing! Have you ever experienced this?
_____
_____
_____

After you've been in God's presence, what lasting difference has it made in your life?
_____
_____
_____

Carol & The Prophetic Dream

During the early morning hours of July 10, 2021, I received the following, short dream:

A woman named Carol I know in real life was standing in a room with her husband. The man who appeared as her husband in the dream is not her husband in real life. He was tall, thin, older, and slumped over when he walked.

In the next scene of the dream, I was standing about 5 feet from Carol who started to sit down in a chair. Her body started to fall forward, and she experienced convulsions. In a crippled state, she fell to the floor as she'd suffered a stroke.

End of dream.

In real life, Carol is a younger woman and in excellent physical health. This dream really startled me, but I knew I'd received it as an important message.

Genesis 40:8 reminds us that all dream interpretations belong to God. When I prayed for the interpretation to this dramatic, strange dream, I felt directed by The Holy Spirit to consult the meaning of Carol's name which is:

"Literal Meaning: Womanly; Song

Suggested Character Quality: Song of Joy

Suggested Lifetime Scripture Verse: John 15:11, 'These things I (Jesus) have spoken to you (His disciples), that My joy may remain in you, and that your joy may be full."

Since Carol suffered a stroke in the dream, she could no longer sing songs of joy.

Just as Jesus talked these matters over with His disciples in John chapter 15, so that His joy would be in them and their joy would be complete, the same applies to us today.

Is there something that's crippling your joy or causing you to "stroke out", so that you are robbed of your joy?

Maintaining Joy In Our Lives

As we continue to read and study Psalm 16, verses 7 – 9 offer additional secrets and instructions on how to maintain joy in our lives:

"I will bless the Lord who has given me counsel;
My heart also instructs me in the night seasons.
I have set the Lord always before me;
Because *He is* at my right hand I shall not be moved.
Therefore my heart is glad, and my glory rejoices;
My flesh also will rest in hope."

Concerning some of the Psalms authored by King David, it's a challenge to discern at exactly what point in his life he penned them. However, from the context of the above scriptures, there are some definite steps we can follow.

#1. Bless our Lord Jesus Who gives us counsel when we ask. (James 3:13-18)

#2. Pray and ask God to give you wisdom and whatever else you need during the night season when your body, soul, mind, and spirit are resting. It's easier to receive during this time than when our spirits are anxious and heavily weighed down. (Philippians 4:6-8)

#3. Setting the Lord before us as our primary focus and keeping Him at our right hand is more than a fantastic visual exercise. It's the enemy of our souls, distractions, battles, diversions, and so forth that divert our attention and continue to give us "spiritual whiplash." King David assures us that because God is at his right hand, he shall not be moved. He'd purposed in his heart to take this stance in the midst of all of his enemies and warfare. Suffice it to say, this works both in times of strife and peace.

#4. A glad heart is our condition and portion if we so choose, and our glory rejoices in our King Jesus.

"But we all, with unveiled face, beholding as in a mirror the glory of the Lord, are being transformed into the same image from glory to glory, just as by the Spirit of the Lord." (2 Corinthians 3:18)

#5. Our flesh can rest in hope just as King David's did. If you read the end of Psalm 16, he knew that God would not leave his soul in Sheol and would show him the path of eternal life which we have through our King Jesus. (Romans 10:9-10)

Prophetic Insights For Daily Living:

(a) In light of the prophetic dream regarding the woman named Carol, is there anything crippling or stifling your joy? If so, God always has a remedy. Seek His face, His word, His Spirit, His Son and answers will surely come forth.

_____
_____
_____

(b) If you're continuing with your prophetic journaling, record what the Lord is showing you and the ways in which He is ministering to you. This will really help in the future as you can revisit what you've recorded if needed.

_____
_____
_____
_____

(c) If you've received the victory over joylessness, consider extending a hand-up to someone in need. Is there someone you can think of right now who could use some help?

_____
_____

(d) God created each of us so uniquely that joy comes to us in many different forms. All of us want to be able to laugh and enjoy our days.

https://sheilaeismann.com/wardrobe-check/

Strength, Dignity & Laughter In Our Immediate Future

May joy in its fullest form be your portion, especially during this bake-oven summer we're experiencing in our neck of the woods or whatever is going on in yours.

"for the kingdom of God is not eating and drinking, but righteousness and peace and joy in the Holy Spirit." (Romans 14:17)

Sheila Eismann, Prophetic Seer, Blogger, Author & Teacher, publishes her weekly blog posts endeavoring to encourage others through God's word. Her writings include teaching and instructions on how to apply prophetic insights for daily living. Please subscribe to receive new blog posts on her website at www.sheilaeismann.com. by clicking the "Subscribe" button in the far upper right-hand corner of her Home webpage.

Growing In Hope – Petal # 7

July 21, 2021
Prophetic Teachings

It could well be that love is the most vital petal on the yellow, supernatural flower that I've been featuring in my blog posts in recent weeks. Since it's important to look for love in all the right places, our first focus is upon God Who is love. (1 John 4:8) From His eternal capacity of limitless love, He encompasses our very being with forgiveness, acceptance, mercy, grace, salvation, hope, the promise of eternal life, and everything else we may ever need. God's love is everlasting.

The epitome of God's love is found in John 3:16, "For God so loved the world that He gave His only begotten Son, that whoever believes in Him should not perish but have everlasting life."

Jesus's love for us was fulfilled by His obedience to His death on the cross. (Philippians 2:8 and 1 John 3:16) Don't you find it fascinating that both of these verses describing God's and Jesus's love contain John 3:16? It's a Biblical twice-speak for double emphasis!

There's no more apt or perfect description of love than the 13th chapter of the book of 1 Corinthians penned by the Apostle Paul. Shall we take a gander at all of love's aspects?

Suffers long
Kind
Does not envy
Does not parade itself
Is not puffed up
Does not behave rudely
Does not seek its own

Is not provoked

Thinks no evil

Does not rejoice in iniquity, but rejoices in the truth

Bears all things

Believes all things

Hopes all things (Emphasis mine)

Endures all things

Never fails

If you're anything like me, you may read this list and consider it virtually impossible to achieve, so why try?

_____
_____
_____

The same thing could be said when Christian women read Proverbs 31 listing all of the attributes of the virtuous wife. These are written for our instruction and help us establish the guidelines and boundaries for life, so we don't just wander aimlessly in a spiritual desert or get sucked into a vacuum without any hope at all.

The above-referenced list from 1 Corinthians 13 goes hand-in-hand with Jesus's greatest command found in Mark 12:30-31,

"And you shall love the Lord your God with all your heart, with all your soul, with all your mind, and with all your strength.' This *is* the first commandment. And the second, like *it, is* this: 'You shall love your neighbor as yourself.' There is no other commandment greater than these."

Loving our neighbor as ourselves is also known as the golden rule. There was a silly one-liner decades ago which read, "He who makes the gold makes the rules." Well, not quite so fast there, sports fans! While this may have been true for those of us who grew up in patriarchal families, it may have been good for a few laughs, but the golden rule is no joke.

As if all of this isn't enough, during Jesus's Sermon on the Mount, He instructs His disciples, "But I say to you, love your enemies, bless those who curse you, do good to those who hate you, and pray for those who spitefully use you and persecute you," (Matthew 5:44)

What if we've made huge mistakes in the area of loving our neighbor, a family member, or anyone in the past? It's never too late to try to remedy the situation, ask for forgiveness, and repair or restore a relationship.

My husband and I recently watched an episode of a series on the History Channel in which a man was at odds his entire life with his parents. His mother died before he could make amends. As he spoke on this show and was trying to process his haunting feelings, it served as a good reminder for all of us. I'm most certainly not making light of this man's misfortune or his choices. The pain was etched on his face and reverberated through his words.

There is a time and season for everything under heaven including a time to love according to Ecclesiastes 3:8a. In one of my previous blog posts, I wrote about the times and seasons of our lives.

https://sheilaeismann.com/spiritual-time/

Four Kinds Of Love

The Bible references four kinds of love which are:

1. *Agape*, the Greek word for which is *agapao* and means concerning people to welcome, to entertain, to be fond of, to love dearly. And, of things, it means to be well pleased, to be contented at or with a thing. This is the type of love referred to in John 3:16, Mark 12:30, and 1 Corinthians 13.
https://www.blueletterbible.org/lexicon/g25/kjv/tr/0-1/

2. *Storge* describes familial love and all that it encompasses. This is one of those instances in scripture wherein the exact word "storge" is not found; however, the opposite of it is used which is *astorgos*. It means without natural affection, unloving, unsociable, or inhuman. There are two Biblical examples of this found in Romans 1:31 and 2 Timothy 3:3.

An example of this type of love can be found in the 11th chapter of John which describes the account of Lazarus's death. Mary and Martha, Lazarus's sisters, have grieved for their brother before Jesus raises him from the dead.
https://www.blueletterbible.org/lexicon/g794/kjv/tr/0-1/

3. *Eros* for which there is no reference found in the New Testament. This is the physical intimacy between a husband and wife. Song of Solomon 1:1-2 in the Old Testament would be a type of this love.

4. *Phileo* love rounds out the list of the four types and refers to love, treating affectionately or kindly, show signs of love, or being fond of doing for someone. John 11:36 depicts this type of love, "Then the Jews said, "See how He (Jesus) loved him (Lazarus)!" This manner of love was so strong and evident that it even ministered to the unbelieving Jews who witnessed it! https://www.blueletterbible.org/lexicon/g5368/kjv/tr/0-1/

God's Everlasting Love Helps In Our Everyday Battles

If you're in any kind of a spiritual battle today, here's a suggested passage of scripture from Romans 8:31-39 to render comfort, perspective, and encouragement:

"What then shall we say to these things? If God *is* for us, who *can be* against us? He who did not spare His own Son, but delivered Him up for us all, how shall He not with Him also freely give us all things? Who shall bring a charge against God's elect? *It is* God who justifies. Who *is* he who condemns? *It is* Christ who died, and furthermore is also risen, who is even at the right hand of God, who also makes intercession for us. Who shall separate us from the love of Christ? *Shall* tribulation, or distress, or persecution, or famine, or nakedness, or peril, or sword? As it is written:

"For Your sake we are killed all day long;
We are accounted as sheep for the slaughter."

Yet in all these things we are more than conquerors through Him who loved us. For I am persuaded that neither death nor life, nor angels nor principalities nor powers, nor things present nor things to come, nor height nor depth, nor any other created thing, shall be able to separate us from the love of God which is in Christ Jesus our Lord."

Prophetic Insights For Daily Living

#1. When you think of the word love, who or what is the first thing that comes to mind?
___
___
___
___

#2. Are you challenged in any of the four kinds of love? If so, which one and why? What could be the root of this?
___
___
___
___

#3. As you read this blog post and study the accompanying scriptures, how have they ministered to you?
___
___

#4. Which type of love is easiest for you to function in, and can you explain why along with giving some contemporary examples?

#5. Do you believe in your heart and mind that God loves you unconditionally with an everlasting love? (Jeremiah 31:3)

#6. 1 John 4 is a fantastic chapter in the New Testament to study in-depth regarding love for God and our fellow man. If you're continuing to write in your prophetic journal, this would be a good passage of scripture to drill deep into, so you can dig out those golden nuggets of truth, encouragement, and instruction.

Hope is like an eternal flower of life that helps to keep us alive in Jesus Christ, our Lord, and Savior. When we combine this with faith and love, it's a winning combination every time. 1 Corinthians 13:13, "And now abide faith, hope, love, these three; but the greatest of these *is* love."

God's everlasting love does indeed change everything!

Sheila Eismann, Prophetic Seer, Blogger, Author & Teacher, publishes her weekly blog posts endeavoring to encourage others through God's word. Her writings include teaching and instructions on how to apply prophetic insights for daily living.

Please subscribe to receive new blog posts on her website at www.sheilaeismann.com. by clicking the "Subscribe" button in the far upper right-hand corner of her Home webpage.

Growing In Hope – Petal # 8

July 26, 2021
Prophetic Teachings

Have you had the opportunity to exercise your "faith muscles" this summer? Since the physical realm mirrors the spiritual one and vice-versa, we must continue to exert our efforts in both areas whether we feel like it or not!

As the wildfires continue to rage in the western United States filling our atmosphere with smoke, it's been a supreme challenge to walk, hike, bicycle, or do almost anything outdoors. Just as obstacles persist in the natural, they do in the spiritual as well.

Faith is the last and 8th petal on the supernatural, yellow flower of hope in the spiritual vision which I received a few weeks ago.

8 is symbolic of new beginnings, a new order of something, new birth, new creation, worship, abounding in strength, regeneration, resurrection, and circumcision of the heart. There are additional meanings, but these are the main ones.

One can only imagine the number of books written and sermons preached on the subject of faith. The Bible is replete with scriptures regarding the same. This alone signals how important faith is to God. Hebrews 11:6 tells us, "But without faith *it is* impossible to please *Him,* for he who comes to God must believe that He is, and *that* He is a rewarder of those who diligently seek Him."

Hope is eagerly waiting with perseverance for what we do not see. (Romans 8:24-25) We cannot have hope without faith.

Faith's Connection To Hope

How is faith connected to hope? Is it possible to have hope if we don't possess faith? Who and/or what are we supposed to place our faith in, especially during the tough times? When we lose faith, we lose hope.

_____
_____
_____

"Why are you cast down, O my soul?
And *why* are you disquieted within me?
Hope in God, for I shall yet praise Him
For the help of His countenance." (Psalm 42:5-6)

In the Bible, hope does not mean hope in the sense of "I hope I win the lottery." It's waiting patiently for something we know we will receive such as eternal life in Christ Jesus our Lord and Savior.

The Swiss Cheese Picture & The Measure Of Our Faith

As Christians, it may appear that our faith is always being tested in one manner or another. While I was waiting on the Lord to author this week's blog post and praying about faith, I saw a large piece of Swiss cheese manifest in the Spirit. I felt like I should ask God, "Will my slice of cheese ever be complete?" I'm confident He doesn't mind silly questions since He has a tremendous sense of humor.

Let's double back to the spiritual meanings for the number eight and marry it up with the Swiss cheese picture, shall we? Ergo, is your faith presently being tested or on trial in any of the following areas?

#1. New beginnings – Do you sense there is going to be a new chapter in your life? If so, what is it? The enemy of our souls really resists when God is about to do something new to help us grow in Him and to advance His kingdom on earth. (Isaiah 43:19)

_____
_____
_____
_____

#2. A new order of something – Is God reordering your life in any area or presenting something new? If our "peace barometer" is out of kilter, it's important to readily accept God's reordering. (Matthew 6:33)

_____
_____
_____
_____

#3. New birth, new creation – Even if we've lived on the earth for decades, God is always doing something new in our lives. New births are needed for areas in which we're deficient or need correction and training for righteousness.

_____
_____
_____
_____

#4. Worship – How's your praise and worship these days? Is it more of a challenge for you to worship God during the "dog days of summer?"

"God *is* Spirit, and those who worship Him must worship in spirit and truth." (John 4:24) When our life is falling apart around us, we definitely need to worship Him!

_____
_____
_____
_____

#5. Abounding in strength – Tapping into God's strength via exercising our faith in Him and His word keeps us spiritually strong. "Finally, my brethren, be strong in the Lord and in the power of His might." (Ephesians 6:10) The Apostle Paul outlines the way we do this is by exercising and waging spiritual warfare. (Ephesians 6:11-18)

_____
_____
_____
_____

#6. Regeneration – of which there are three basic definitions: https://www.merriam-webster.com/dictionary/regenerate

(a) formed or created again

(b) spiritually reborn or converted

(c) restored to a better, higher, or more worthy state

#7. If we've been pummeled or flattened on the battlefield, our faith may need to be formed or created once again. In supreme spiritual boxing matches where we've been knocked out cold, Dr. Jesus comes in and quickly revives us if we draw near to Him and stay there. (Jeremiah 29:12-14 and James 4:8)

#8. Resurrection – this sort of goes hand-in-hand with regeneration. Our entire Christian walk and/or experience can slide into an endless wasteland during a spiritual tsunami. There's no guilt or shame in running to the Lord Who is a strong tower and allowing Him to fully resurrect us. (Proverbs 18:10)

#9. Circumcision of the heart – As part of the New Covenant, believers undergo a circumcision of the heart in the Spirit wherein the flesh of sin, unbelief, etc. is removed from them. (Romans 2:29) As painful as this can be as our flesh screams loudly, it truly is for our good and overall spiritual health.

A Walk With The Heroes of Faith

If, while you're reading this blog post you might be "down in the dumps," please open your Bible and read the 11th chapter of Hebrews. This quickly puts faith into perspective. The "cha-ching" of the entire matter appears in verse 39, "And all these (the aforementioned in Hebrews Chapter 11), having obtained a good testimony through faith, did not receive the promise."

What was the promise?

_____
_____
_____
_____

It was the promise, guarantee, and prophetic fulfillment of the coming Messiah, Jesus Christ of Nazareth. (Isaiah 7:14 and 40:3; Jeremiah 31:31-34; Micah 5:2; Matthew 1:1 and 23, 11:2-3, 16:20; John 4:25, 7:42, 20:31; Luke 9:20, 23:2 and 35; and 1 Peter 1:18-20)

Praise be unto God that Jesus was born, fulfilled His earthly assignment, was crucified, resurrected, and now sits at the right hand of God the Father in heaven! (Psalm 110:1 and Hebrews 1:3) This is the true foundation upon which we can exercise our faith and let it soar to the heavens.

Who is your favorite hero in this chapter and why? Which one can you relate to the most? Would you like to be able to sit down and have a conversation with him or her? Be patient as you'll be able to do that in heaven.

_____
_____
_____
_____

Here's a blog post I authored a few months ago titled "The Maturity Is In The Waiting." There may be some suggestions therein as you read through it to help increase your faith in God, Jesus, and The Holy Spirit.

https://sheilaeismann.com/freedom-from-anxiety/

The Maturity Is In The Waiting

Prophetic Insights For Daily Living

#1. What is your favorite faith scripture?

_____
_____
_____

#2. Where are you in your faith journey, i.e., are you a new believer standing upon Romans 10:17, "So then faith *comes* by hearing, and hearing by the word of God?" There's a major clue in this verse for all believers irrespective of where we are on our spiritual journey. To remain strong in our Lord Jesus and maintain our faith in Him, we must stay in His word. Believe it and appropriate it.

#3. What kinds of things deplete your faith? To shore it up, how have you gained the victory, or what strategies could you share with other believers?

#4. Do you find it a challenge to share your faith? If so, one suggestion is to practice giving your testimony of how you came to Christ and accepted Him as your personal Lord and Savior. (Romans 10:9-10) You don't even need an audience to do this as you can look into the mirror and talk to yourself if necessary. Frequency and repetition will lessen your fears and embolden you.

#5. Pray and ask The Holy Spirit to give you the gift of faith if you are lacking in faith and fighting any battle right now. Ask Him to help you exercise your faith. (1 Corinthians 12:9)

Wrapping up our 8 weeks of meditating upon the 8 petals of the supernatural flower of hope, which one has been your favorite or ministered to you the most? Hope is contagious in a good way. When I meet or speak with one of my prayer partners each week, she radiates hope and helps to keep my "hope barometer" rising. Despite her personal challenges, her hopes are riding high in God and His word.

Jesus is the hope of the world. Since we are His kingdom workers, may we continue to spread His hope to everyone we encounter each day! (Romans 16:3,12; Philippians 4:3 and 3 John 8)

Sheila Eismann, Prophetic Seer, Blogger, Author & Teacher, publishes her weekly blog posts endeavoring to encourage others through God's word. Her writings include teaching and instructions on how to apply prophetic insights for daily living.

Please subscribe to receive new blog posts on her website at www.sheilaeismann.com. by clicking the "Subscribe" button in the far upper right-hand corner of her Home webpage.

Sheila Eismann

The Coyote, Peter & Summer

August 3, 2021
Prophetic Dreams

What crafty creature emerges from a hot rock setting that causes you to wait and be of good courage? For this particular spiritual riddle which is a type of statement, question, or phrase causing you to think, I've already given you a major clue! Let's unpack my recent prophetic dream involving the coyote, Peter & Summer, shall we?

Do you enjoy solving a spiritual riddle and/or puzzle? What's the basic difference between the two? First, let's take a gander at the definition of a riddle:

1: a mystifying, misleading, or puzzling question posed as a problem to be solved or guessed: conundrum, an enigma.

2: something or someone difficult to understand.

https://www.merriam-webster.com/dictionary/riddle

A riddle has a correct answer, which someone must answer after deliberating on it and applying logical reasoning.

A puzzle is more a type of game, toy, structure, or problem, whose purpose is to test someone's knowledge, ingenuity, thinking and processing skills, etc.

When the prophetic dream opened, a woman was riding in the back of an older model, light-sage-green-colored truck with a wooden bed. It was more along the lines of a type that was used decades ago on farms during harvest season. The truck was headed up a hill on a dirt road, and the driver was accelerating way too fast for safe travel. I have no idea who was driving the truck as this was not revealed to me in the dream.

Four dead coyotes were laying on the weathered, wooden bed near the cab of the truck. Peter was riding in the back with the woman, and he was bending down at his knees looking at something near the tailgate. He was wearing navy-blue-colored summer shorts and a white t-shirt. The woman wore summer attire as well.

Some scenes in dreams are supernatural in origin. It isn't that the events depicted therein couldn't happen in real life because they could. Having said that, the woman picked up a 5th dead coyote that just suddenly appeared in the dream to toss it from the rapidly moving truck.

Suddenly, the dream flipped in a nano-second to where the woman tossed Peter from the truck instead of the 5th dead coyote.

Even though I was in a very deep sleep, I distinctly remember seeing Peter flying out the rear into midair and the blood around the dead coyote's mouth as the woman laid it next to the other four on the wooden truck bed. I never did see Peter land on the side of the road or onto the desert floor.

After the truck had traveled for a few more minutes up the hill, the woman in the back decided to knock on the back window to try to get the driver's attention to stop the truck. She was unsuccessful in doing this.

In the last scene of the dream, I was running down the same road the truck had traveled uphill with a woman named Summer who I know in real life.

Both of us were frantically calling Peter's name hoping he would emerge from the desert setting of juniper, mahogany, and pine trees, rabbitbrush, skunk cabbage, milkweed, and yellow wildflowers along the sides of the road. We ran for quite some time but never did find him.

Then I awakened from this dream with my heart racing. This was one of those kinds of dreams where I was in a deep REM, but it was as if I was wide awake the entire time. I could hear myself yelling with everything that was within me.

Coyotes

When you think of this animal, what comes to mind? Have you ever seen one in its natural setting? Why do you think several of them appeared in the dream?

_____
_____
_____

My daddy trapped coyotes in the extreme southwestern part of our state for decades. He did this to help sheep and cattle ranchers since coyotes can wreak havoc on flocks and herds. He had trapping licenses in two adjoining states and was very successful at what he did. The ranchers and farmers were most appreciative. Daddy had studied these cunning, crafty creatures and had a real talent for setting the snares perfectly to catch a lot of them.

If you encounter some coyotes in your neighborhood, make sure to protect your children and pets. They can become very comfortable in certain regions and become suddenly aggressive with stalking other animals and people.

Some symbolisms for coyotes are sly, tricky, crafty, cunning, double-minded, aggressive behavior, not trustworthy, and predator.

Peter – The Rock

The picture accompanying my weekly blog post shows a coyote standing close to an igneous rock which is typically found in a desert setting such as the geographic region in which I live.

The meaning of Peter's name in this dream is most instructive:

"Peter

Literal Meaning: Rock

Suggested Character Quality: Strong in spirit

Suggested Lifetime Scripture Verse: Psalm 27:14,

'Wait on the Lord;
Be of good courage,
And He shall strengthen your heart;
Wait, I say, on the Lord!'"

In the dream, the woman threw Peter out of the truck into midair and replaced him with a dead coyote. Even though this may sound morbid, perhaps she thought she was being clever and relying upon her own understanding (symbolism for a coyote) and not waiting on the Lord to give her courage and to strengthen her heart (meaning for Peter's name).

It's also significant that she waited for a few minutes before trying to get the driver's attention to pull off the side of the road, so they could double back and look for Peter.

The five dead coyotes signal the woman's five futile attempts at whatever she was trying to achieve or do through her own craftiness or strength. Five represents God's grace to man and man's responsibility. It also symbolizes abundance, favor, and redemption.

Double Summer

My friend Summer, who spells her name Sommer, is a dedicated, lovey Christian woman with a prophetic gifting. Her appearance in this dream has a double meaning in that it indicates the summer season in which we now find ourselves and gives assistance with decoding the prophetic dream and riddle. In other words, this is a word in due season for this summer for those who need and/or want to apply it to their life.

Prophetic Insights For Daily Living

A. Are you waiting on the Lord for anything – (the accompanying scripture verse to the meaning of Peter's name)? Most people I know are definitely in this camp right now during summer.

B. The Holy Spirit recently impressed upon me **5** things from Psalm 37:3-4 that we can implement while we're waiting. I guess you could say these would replace the **5** "dead things" from my recent, prophetic dream.

"Trust in the Lord, and do good;
Dwell in the land, and feed on His faithfulness.
Delight yourself also in the Lord,
And He shall give you the desires of your heart."

1 – Trust in the LORD (Proverbs 3:5-6)

2 – Do good (Galatians 6:9)

3 – Dwell (Numbers 33:53)

4 – Feed (1 Corinthians 1:9)

5 – Delight (Isaiah 58:14)

What additional companion scriptures would you add to the aforementioned list?

Think of practical ways in which you can implement the golden instructions outlined in these two verses from Psalm 37. Let's just take number 2 as an example which is **do good**. If we purpose in our hearts to do something good and kind for someone as often as we can, God will surely give us the opportunity. It doesn't take solving a spiritual riddle to accomplish this, thankfully.

Which one on this list is the most challenging for you? Doubling back to the woman in the dream, it's obvious she severely lacked trust in God and grew impatient, or else she would not have thrown Peter out the back of a fast-moving truck bed! We develop strength and trust in the Lord when we wait upon Him.

https://sheilaeismann.com/wardrobe-check/

C. As you ponder and pray into this prophetic dream, what has The Holy Spirit quickened unto you?

_____

_____

_____

D. Even though Summer and I did not find Peter in the dream, we were searching for him. We know in real life that we will find God when we search for Him with all of our heart according to Jeremiah 29:13.

Summer and I will be encouraged and strengthened in real life this summer as we wait on our Lord Jesus.

Years ago, I had the pure delight of assisting with a Vacation Bible School way down in the desert. One of the songs we taught the little kiddos was, "When we walk with the Lord, we don't get bored!"

This recent prophetic dream was fun to flesh out. I hope you enjoyed it, too.

Even though we're experiencing a severe drought in the western United States this summer, we can still choose to trust the Lord.

"Blessed *is* the man who trusts in the Lord,
And whose hope is the Lord.
For he shall be like a tree planted by the waters,
Which spreads out its roots by the river,
And will not fear when heat comes;

But its leaf will be green,

And will not be anxious in the year of drought,

Nor will cease from yielding fruit." (Jeremiah 17:7-8)

Sheila Eismann, Prophetic Seer, Blogger, Author & Teacher, publishes her weekly blog posts endeavoring to encourage others through God's word. Her writings include teaching and instructions on how to apply prophetic insights for daily living.

Please subscribe to receive new blog posts on her website at www.sheilaeismann.com. by clicking the "Subscribe" button in the far upper right-hand corner of her Home webpage.

Sheila Eismann

Be Filled & Poured Out!

August 10, 2021
Prophetic Teachings

The western region of our country is currently experiencing innumerable fires and severe droughts which have led to some ranchers having to sell their herds early because there's no water to raise feed for them. Also, farmers and orchardists will not have full crops to harvest late this summer or fall. Within the city limits, we are being asked to conserve as much water as we can as lawns turn from plush green to dead brown and the leaves on the trees grow limp. The land is parched, and the desert is screaming for a long, sustained drink!

Today's newspaper headlines read, "Major drought in Idaho could last years, water manager says."

https://www.idahopress.com/news/state/major-drought-in-idaho-could-last-years-water-manager-says/article_9a23b7ad-9b56-526b-83bf-d55febadcc11.html

When I was a young girl growing up on Sage Creek Farms, I liked to watch for small patches of dry ground that had been irrigated in the spring. It was hard and cracked and looked like pieces of a jig-saw puzzle. While my daddy had us herding cows on our ditch banks and pastures, I would entertain myself by trying to carefully pry the pieces loose and fashion a new puzzle of my own. I was rarely successful in doing this, but it did help to pass the time of day until it was time to drive the cows back to the barn for the evening milking.

As I've continued to pray and ask God to send rain to quench the fires and help the firefighters, the picture I have received in the Spirit is the same one I saw as a young girl on our farm.

In some of my previous blog posts, I've mentioned that the natural oftentimes parallels the spiritual and vice-versa. When we study the New Testament, we observe that Jesus taught in parables using the elements of everyday agrarian society. An example of this would be the Parable of the Sower found in Matthew 13:1-9,

"On the same day Jesus went out of the house and sat by the sea. And great multitudes were gathered together to Him, so that He got into a boat and sat; and the whole multitude stood on the shore.

Then He spoke many things to them in parables, saying: 'Behold, a sower went out to sow. And as he sowed, some *seed* fell by the wayside; and the birds came and devoured them. Some fell on stony places, where they did not have much earth; and they immediately sprang up because they had no depth of earth. But when the sun was up they were scorched, and because they had no root they withered away. And some fell among thorns, and the thorns sprang up and choked them. But others fell on good ground and yielded a crop: some a hundredfold, some sixty, some thirty. He who has ears to hear, let him hear!'"

Who is the sower? What is the seed?

___

___

___

This parable is explained in Matthew 13:18-23. I would encourage you to read this to see how The Holy Spirit speaks to you and what He downloads to your spirit.

Obviously, we cannot produce rain, and when the reservoirs and rivers run dry, there's no irrigation availability. The Bible tells us that God has rain stored in His storehouses just like He does hail, wind, snow, etc. (Leviticus 26:4; Deuteronomy 11:10-15, 28:12; Job 5:10, 26:8-9, 36:26-33, 38:22; Proverbs 3:19-20; Psalm 135:7, 147:8, 148:8; Jeremiah 5:24, 10:13; Matthew 5:45; and Acts 14:17)

Rivers of Living Water

It's not only the ground that's bone dry, but some people are, too. Let's revisit the 7th chapter of the Book of John in the New Testament. Jesus is walking in Galilee, and the Jews' Feast of Tabernacles is at hand. In the middle of this feast, Jesus enters the temple to teach wherein he encounters the backlash of the religious leaders despite others present who did believe in Him.

Can you only imagine having been present inside the temple when Jesus unleashed the following?

"On the last day, that great *day* of the feast, Jesus stood and cried out, saying, 'If anyone thirsts, let him come to Me and drink. He who believes in Me, as the Scripture has said, out of his heart will flow rivers of living water.' But this He spoke concerning the Spirit, whom those believing in Him would receive; for the Holy Spirit was not yet *given,* because Jesus was not yet glorified." (John 7:37-39)

I would love to have been there. Talk about dramatic!

When we accept Jesus Christ as our personal Lord and Savior (Romans 10:9-10), we are indwelt with The Holy Spirit of God. (John 14:17 and 1 Corinthians 12:13)

A Christian's heart is the Holy Spirit's home. With God's help, we can make a beautiful place for The Holy Spirit to reside.

"Now He who establishes us with you in Christ and has anointed us *is* God, who also has sealed us and given us the Spirit in our hearts as a guarantee." (Ephesians 1:13-14 and 2 Corinthians 1:21-22)
However, there's an ongoing need to be filled, so we can be poured out as the rivers of living water flow from us to others. (Ephesians 5:18)

Never Be Thirsty Again

In the 4th chapter of John, there's the account of a Samaritan woman who meets her Messiah. That was a divine Holy Spirit set-up for the ages! A tired Jesus sat down at Jacob's well about the sixth hour when a Samaritan woman came to draw water. Jesus asked her for a drink, and she was quite startled since Jews have no dealings with Samaritans.

Jesus continues His dialogue with the Samaritan woman wherein He speaks of living water. In John 4:13-14, "Jesus answered and said to her, 'Whoever drinks of this water will thirst again, but whoever drinks of the water that I shall give him will never thirst. But the water that I shall give him will become in him a fountain of water springing up into everlasting life.'"

Because we can have the promise and guarantee of The Holy Spirit dwelling within us (Ephesians 1:13-14), we have help to avoid becoming spiritually thirsty again.

Poured Out As A Drink Offering

The Apostle Paul speaks of being poured out as a drink offering in Philippians 2:17-18,

"Yes, and if I am being poured out *as a drink offering* on the sacrifice and service of your faith, I am glad and rejoice with you all. For the same reason, you also be glad and rejoice with me."

Since the church at Philippi was offering something to God, Paul wanted to encourage the believers in Christ further by saying that he would like to pour himself out as a drink offering upon their sacrifice. As Christians, we can greatly encourage one another by sharing our experiences of what Jesus has done for us. It's in this manner that we "pour out," but we must first be filled with the Holy Spirit to do so.

One of my favorite things is to listen to personal testimonies of how people come to Christ and accept Him as their personal Lord and Savior. This is such a faith builder!

Prophetic Insights For Daily Living

#1. Please join me in continuing to pray for God to send rain to help put the fires out and aid all of humanity affected by the drought and fires, wildlife, ranchers, farmers, and all livestock.

#2. An additional prayer is for God to pour out His Holy Spirit gifts in a greater measure upon believers in Christ everywhere – not just in the western part of the United States. (1 Corinthians Chapter 12)

#3. How does The Holy Spirit help you in your everyday life?
_____
_____
_____
_____

#4. Are you in need of any of the spiritual gifts mentioned in the New Testament such as a word of wisdom, word of knowledge, healing, or miracles? Pray and ask God for them to be released for whatever situation is needed.

_____
_____
_____
_____

#5. Do you feel spiritually thirsty? If so, here are some suggestions to quench your spiritual thirst: read and study your Bible, praise and worship the Lord, attend your local church fellowship and Bible study group, connect with a prayer partner, fast, and pray. What other recommendations could you offer?

_____
_____
_____
_____

#6. Have you ever shared your testimony of how you came to Christ and accepted Him as your personal Lord and Savior? If not, pray and ask the Lord to allow you to do so.

_____
_____
_____
_____

#7. Look for ways and divine appointments to render kindness, blessings, encouragement, love, and goodness. Some people will latch onto these like it's their last drink of water.

As 2020 was winding down, I titled one of my weekly blog posts, "Kindness ~ An Invaluable Currency."

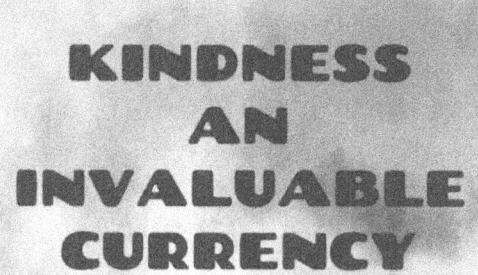

To revisit it, here's the link: https://sheilaeismann.com/spiritual-currency/

The natural rivers out west may be running dry, but as Christians, we have an ongoing promise and guarantee of The Holy Spirit from Whom there will always be a release of rivers of living water flowing from our hearts which we can share with those who we encounter daily to bring life and hope to them.

Sheila Eismann, Prophetic Seer, Blogger, Author & Teacher, publishes her weekly blog posts endeavoring to encourage others through God's word. Her writings include teaching and instructions on how to apply prophetic insights for daily living.

Please subscribe to receive new blog posts on her website at www.sheilaeismann.com. by clicking the "Subscribe" button in the far upper right-hand corner of her Home webpage.

Drink From Wisdom's Cup
August 17, 2021
Prophetic Visions

What is your favorite daily beverage? Is it coffee, tea, soda, water, mineral water, milk, chocolate milk, or something else? Oh, so many choices! We're experiencing an unusual, prolonged drought in our area, so I'm trying to drink as much water as I can to stay hydrated.

During my time of seeking the Lord and praying, the Spirit realm opened, and I saw an antique, gold-colored goblet with 7 ruby-red colored diamonds on the front of it. Engraved on the base in the matching red tone was the word ***Wisdom***.

Immediately upon receiving this vision, I heard, "Drink from Wisdom's cup." The Holy Spirit impressed upon me that this is to be a daily drink or intaking as we strive to be wise.

Several scriptures were quickened unto me:

#1. Proverbs 4:7 (NIV)

"The beginning of wisdom is this: Get wisdom. Though it cost all you have, get understanding."

We're living in the days of increased physical hyper-inflation which parallels the spiritual realm as well. It's as if the physical price of everything is rising but so is the noise decibel level on all fronts. False and worldly wisdom is hyperinflated, too.

Wisdom has her own voice which can be heard above all others, but we have to shut the white noise of the world out so that we can hear her.

"She (wisdom) cries out from the highest places of the city,
'Whoever *is* simple, let him turn in here!'
As for him who lacks understanding, she says to him,
'Come, eat of my bread
And drink of the wine I have mixed.
Forsake foolishness and live,
And go in the way of understanding.'" (Proverbs 9:3b-6)

The inference and logical progression are that first wisdom needs to be attained, and then we proceed to gain an understanding of the wisdom that has been given to us. An analogy would be that of building a house. The wisdom portion of it is the blueprint or basic draft design even if it's something like a simple, one-room log cabin in a forest. Once that is completed, the building of the structure begins which is the equivalent of going in the way of understanding.

What example could you supply to illustrate this point?

_____
_____
_____
_____

Stated another way, there's usually a wise way and/or a foolish way to proceed in every matter or decision. If we proceed without any wisdom, the results could be disastrous or at least less than favorable. As disciples of Christ, we must consider the long game in every matter.

#2. Proverbs 9:10

"The fear of the Lord *is* the beginning of wisdom,
 And the knowledge of the Holy One *is* understanding."

Thankfully, the Lord did not leave us in a lurch concerning how to start attaining wisdom in the first place. There is a positive and a negative fear of the Lord which speaks for itself. The positive aspect is a holy, reverential one wherein we place Him first in our lives and adhere to and study His holy word through which we learn about His attributes and kingdom.

When we read and study the Bible, it's crystal clear how we're to live out each day. We're unable to do it on our own through the flesh. God, Jesus, and The Holy Spirit offer their supernatural help 24/7.

#3. Proverbs 14:33(a)

"Wisdom rests in the heart of him who has understanding."

This verse illustrates the beautiful partnership between wisdom and understanding. It also shows us that wisdom desires to take up residence within us.

If someone parked in the book of Proverbs and read only that book alone for a few days, a follow-up conversation would be most enlightening as to how much wisdom and understanding had been gained that was not necessarily present beforehand.

The 7 Diamonds

The 7 diamonds which appeared on the front of the antique goblet are quite fascinating.

The number 7 is symbolic of maturity, satiated, the swearing of an oath, sufficiency, promise (the 7 colors of the rainbow), wisdom, revelation, divine perfection, completion, blessings, or a specific number of something such as 7 days, months, years, decades, people, etc.

A cup speaks of our portion, blessings, covenant, salvation or redemption, God's will in our lives, resurrection and eternal life, our responsibility connected with the call of God on our lives, and God's wrath or fury being poured out. There are additional meanings, but these are some of the main ones.

I deem the one which marries up the closest with this prophetic vision is ascertaining God's will in our lives and discerning the call of God upon our lives and our responsibility to respond accordingly.

James 3:17

A couple of days after receiving this vision, the Holy Spirit directed me to the third chapter of the book of James in the New Testament. As my spiritual eyes were opened, I gleaned there are 7 spiritual attributes to heavenly wisdom which are:

Pure

Peaceable

Gentle

Willing to yield

Full of mercy and good fruits

Without partiality

Without hypocrisy

These 7 diamonds stand in stark contrast to the earthly and demonic wisdom listed in James 3:13-16,

"Who *is* **wise and understanding** among you? Let him show by good conduct *that* his works *are done* in the meekness of wisdom. But if you have bitter envy and self-seeking in your hearts, do not boast and lie against the truth. This wisdom does not descend from above, but *is* earthly, sensual, demonic. For where envy and self-seeking *exist,* confusion and every evil thing *are* there." (Emphasis mine to reinforce the partnership of wisdom and understanding once again.)

The Breastplate Of The High Priest

During Old Testament days, whoever had been appointed the High Priest in Israel at that time wore the breastplate bearing the precious stones representing the 12 tribes of Israel. (Exodus 28:15-21)

The tribe of Gad was represented by the diamond. The Gadites were supreme warriors who would cross the Jordan River during the flood stage to go after their enemies to subdue them. Two stellar examples of this tribe are Elijah and Jephthah both of whom were instrumental in helping to execute the justice of the Lord.

The sardius or red stone on the high priest's breastplate was indicative of the tribe of Judah which means praise. Jesus descended from this lineage. (Genesis 49:10, Isaiah 11:1, Matthew 1:1-16 and Luke 3:23-38)

After we accept Jesus Christ as our Lord and Savior, we become kings and priests in His kingdom. (1 Peter 2:9 and Revelation 5:10) We are not required to wear a breastplate such as Moses's brother Aaron did in the Old Testament, but we can continue to be "Gadites" or warriors for Christ and praise King Jesus all the time!

An excellent read on the garments worn by the high priest during Old Testament times was written by C. W. Slemming and titled *These Are The Garments*.

https://www.amazon.com/These-Are-Garments-Charles-Slemming/dp/0875085075/ref=sr_1_1?dchild=1&keywords=these+are+the+garments&qid=1629059917&sr=8-1

As the calendar turned to 2021, I wrote a helpful blog post regarding attaining a heart of wisdom:

https://sheilaeismann.com/heart-of-wisdom/

The Open Gate

Prophetic Insights For Daily Living

#1. There are going to be practical and spiritual things the Lord is going to require us to do as it pertains to wisdom and understanding. Make a list of these as they are revealed to you, the date and time they appear, and act upon each one.

_____
_____
_____
_____

#2. During your quiet time, pray and ask the Lord to increase your wisdom and understanding if needed as no one person possesses all of the wisdom and understanding they will ever need throughout his or her lifetime. There is much assurance which can be found in James 1:5, "If any of you lacks wisdom, let him ask of God, who gives to all liberally and without reproach, and it will be given to him."

_____
_____
_____

#3. Do you have any major or minor decisions to make? You can plug in the "7 diamonds" as you drink daily from Wisdom's cup. This will help you make the correct decision which will bear good fruit in the immediate or distant future.

_____
_____

#4. Have you been drinking from a different cup, so to speak, such as a "worldly cup?" It's never too late to discard the latter, and order one from heaven. While I realize this is a supernatural act, it positively does work!

#5. Study your favorite Biblical character whether Old or New Testament other than Jesus, of course. Note the wise and unwise decisions he or she made and the end results as the Bible tells us that all scripture was written for our example. (Romans 15:4) In doing this, we aren't judging the former life of anyone, but definitely learning from their choices which were recorded for a divine purpose.

#6. Choose to do a topical study on the subject of wisdom. The Bible has a lot to say about this subject.

If you or your loved ones have not yet accepted Jesus Christ as your personal Lord and Savior, it's never too late to make this decision. Eternity is a very long time. Romans 10:9-10 is the road map, "that if you confess with your mouth the Lord Jesus and believe in your heart that God has raised Him from the dead, you will be saved. For with the heart one believes unto righteousness, and with the mouth confession is made unto salvation."

Jesus's instructions to His disciples in His Sermon on the Mount included,

"Therefore do not worry, saying, 'What shall we eat?' or 'What shall we drink?' or 'What shall we wear?' For after all these things the Gentiles seek. For your heavenly Father knows that you need all these things. But seek first the kingdom of God and His righteousness, and all these things shall be added to you." (Matthew 6:31-33)

In Christendom, this is one of the most challenging places to live where we don't worry about a single, solitary thing and trust God for everything as we seek first His Kingdom and righteousness.

If we drink from Wisdom's cup daily, surely this will help our trust factor as we reap the spiritual and physical benefits. Drink up!

Sheila Eismann, Prophetic Seer, Blogger, Author & Teacher, publishes her weekly blog posts endeavoring to encourage others through God's word. Her writings include teaching and instructions on how to apply prophetic insights for daily living.

Please subscribe to receive new blog posts on her website at www.sheilaeismann.com by clicking the "Subscribe" button in the far upper right-hand corner of her Home webpage.

Sheila Eismann

The Covenant Academy On Deuteronomy Street

August 23, 2021
Prophetic Dreams

In a recent unique dream, I'd gone to see an elderly lady. I have no idea who she is, and she did not resemble anyone I know. When the prophetic dream opened, I was visiting inside her living room as she sat on her couch. This woman had grey hair and appeared to be in her mid to late '80s. She was wearing a light blue, long-sleeved knit top and dark blue slacks. I sat cross-legged on the floor in front of her and was the same age in the dream as I am in real life now. I was dressed in a summer top and shorts and was holding my black, leather fanny pack on my lap. The woman said, "I'm teaching at The Covenant Academy on Deuteronomy Street."

Scene #2 of the dream continued where I was walking inside a city and crossing from one street to another in pursuit of locating the academy. The dream ended before I arrived there.

As I've pondered and prayed into this dream, what the woman spoke to me is so unique. I was unable to locate a street in the real world bearing the name Deuteronomy. Following this dream, I felt led to read The Fifth Book of Moses called Deuteronomy.

The name Deuteronomy means "the second law." The book does not contain this; however, God used Moses to explain the law as it was revealed on Mt. Sinai to the second generation of the Israelites. Also, he recounted Israel's history up to the point of entering the Promised Land and challenged those entering the land to renew their covenant with God.

Per God's command, Moses wrote down the words of the law, gave them to the priests, and charged them with safekeeping. He commanded the priests to read the words every seven years. (Deuteronomy 31:9-13) The major emphasis of the book is the covenant between the Israelites and God.

The woman in the dream was teaching at The Covenant Academy on Deuteronomy Street which is almost a Biblical twice speak in and of itself since Moses emphasized the subject of the covenant so much in this Biblical book. Deuteronomy 27:1-26 outlines the renewal of the covenant in Canaan under Joshua who was anointed to take Moses's place once Israel entered the Promised Land.

Prophetic Symbolisms In This Dream:

#1. A fanny pack is what I use for my purse these days while still navigating the parameters of Covid since I can just fasten it around my waist. A purse symbolizes a person's heart as that's the place where values are stored, faith, security, finances, or identity.

#2. It's sort of odd that I was sitting on the floor looking at the woman rather than in a chair as there were chairs present in her living room. The floor indicates a foundation that lines up with the covenant because every spiritual covenant has a spiritual foundation.

#3. Grey hair – The older woman had grey hair which represents maturity, wisdom, and someone deserving of respect. When the grey-haired woman in the dream spoke, it reinforces 1 Corinthians 1-13. We are to learn from what happened to those who broke their covenant with God that Moses outlined in the book of Deuteronomy. When they disobeyed God, the whole nation went into exile into Assyria and Babylon.

#4. The summer clothing I was wearing in the dream is one of the outfits I have been wearing lately, so this speaks to me of being a "now word" as opposed to one in the future.

#5. Covenant speaks for itself which means an agreement between parties.

#6. Academy is a school or place of learning. In this dream, I did not arrive there, but I was in pursuit of locating it. Also, the academy was located on Deuteronomy Street which is the place to learn about the covenant in the book of Deuteronomy.

#7. A street is symbolized by several things: a person's path of life, gathering place, the future, the spiritual condition of a city, or public announcement. How is the spiritual condition of your city these days?

The Old & The New Covenants

Deuteronomy 4:12-13 outlines the Old Covenant:

"And the Lord spoke to you (the Israelites) out of the midst of the fire. You heard the sound of the words, but saw no form; *you* only *heard* a voice. So He declared to you His covenant which He commanded you to perform, the Ten Commandments; and He wrote them on two tablets of stone."

When God delivered the first covenant, the Israelites could not see Him but only heard His voice.

There was a guarantee of the New Covenant in Jeremiah 31:31-34:

"Behold, the days are coming, says the Lord, when I will make a new covenant with the house of Israel and with the house of Judah— not according to the covenant that I made with their fathers in the day *that* I took them by the hand to lead them out of the land of Egypt, My covenant which they broke, though I was a husband to them, says the Lord. But this *is* the covenant that I will make with the house of Israel after those days, says the Lord: I will put My law in their minds, and write it on their hearts; and I will be their God, and they shall be My people. No more shall every man teach his neighbor, and every man his brother, saying, 'Know the Lord,' for they all shall know Me, from the least of them to the greatest of them, says the Lord. For I will forgive their iniquity, and their sin I will remember no more."

Some present-day Christians believe that the Old Testament no longer applies to us today since we are living under the New Covenant. The Apostle Paul reminds us in Romans 15:4, "For whatever things were written before were written for our learning, that we through the patience and comfort of the Scriptures might have hope." The "before" portion of this verse would certainly include the Old Testament. In addition, the above verse from Jeremiah is repeated in Hebrews 8:7-13.

Jesus is our mediator of the New Covenant (Hebrews 9:15) and came to fulfill all of the law and the prophets. (Matthew 5:17-20) All of the law and prophets are summed up via Matthew 22:37-40,

"Jesus said to him (a Pharisee, lawyer), 'You shall love the Lord your God with all your heart, with all your soul, and with all your mind.' This is *the* first and great commandment. And *the* second *is* like it: 'You shall love your neighbor as yourself.' On these two commandments hang all the Law and the Prophets."

We're presently under the covenant of grace but that doesn't mean we can't break that covenant. Jesus stated in John 14:15, "If you love Me, keep My commandments." But He also warned in Matthew 7:21-23, "Not everyone who says to Me, 'Lord, Lord,' shall enter the kingdom of heaven, but he who does the will of My Father in heaven. Many will say to Me in that day, 'Lord, Lord, have we not prophesied in Your name, cast out demons in Your name, and done many wonders in Your name?' And then I will declare to them, 'I never knew you; depart from Me, you who practice lawlessness!'" (2 Timothy 2:12 and Titus 1:16)

Going Your Own Way

https://sheilaeismann.com/dangers-of-distractions/

Prophetic Insights For Daily Living:

#1. In the first portion of Deuteronomy, Moses recounts Israel's path from leaving Egypt to entering the Promised Land. Egypt represents the world. Retrace your steps before your salvation of all that God has done for you to take you from the kingdom of darkness into His kingdom and give praise unto Him!

#2. Deuteronomy 4:23 – Moses reminds the Israelites to not forget the covenant and form idols in our lives.

#3. Deuteronomy 7:9 – There's a wonderful promise for 1,000 generations for those who keep God's covenant.

#4. Israel was poised to enter the land of their promised inheritance. What "new land or opportunity" is the Lord placing before you to possess with His help, instructions, and blessings?

_____
_____
_____
_____

#5. Deuteronomy 10:11-12 – God requires the same thing from us today as He did from Israel because it's for our good. It's as if time has not advanced one second.

#6. Deuteronomy 11:7 – the eyes of the Israelites had seen every great act of the Lord which He did. What great acts and answers to prayer has the Lord done for you?

_____
_____
_____
_____

#7. Deuteronomy 13:5 – One repetitive theme in this entire book is God's requirement to put away the evil from our midst. There's a clarion call to examine our hearts and do the same.

#8. Deuteronomy 20:1-4 – God's assurance that He is with us in our battles, and He will fight for us.

The elderly woman who was teaching at The Covenant Academy on Deuteronomy Street symbolizes how important covenant is to God, and this is why she was teaching it. She spoke this in the dream to reinforce the importance to me. Deuteronomy Street takes us back to the covenant that Israel made with God in the book of Deuteronomy which is the 5th book of Moses.

5 is symbolic of God's grace to man and man's responsibility. And even though the Israelites were God's chosen people, when they broke their covenant with Him, they were sent into captivity. There are still consequences to all of us today for breaking our covenant with God as it's a mutual covenant.

As you read and study the book of Deuteronomy along with this prophetic unique dream, what other dream interpretations would you add, and what have you gleaned?

_____
_____
_____
_____
_____
_____
_____
_____
_____
_____

We can be encouraged from Deuteronomy 30:14 and Romans 10:8, "But the word *is* very near you, in your mouth and in your heart, that you may do it."

Sheila Eismann, Prophetic Seer, Blogger, Author & Teacher, publishes her weekly blog posts endeavoring to encourage others through God's word. Her writings include teaching and instructions on how to apply prophetic insights for daily living.

Please subscribe to receive new blog posts on her website at www.sheilaeismann.com by clicking the "Subscribe" button in the far upper right-hand corner of her Home webpage.

Sheila Eismann

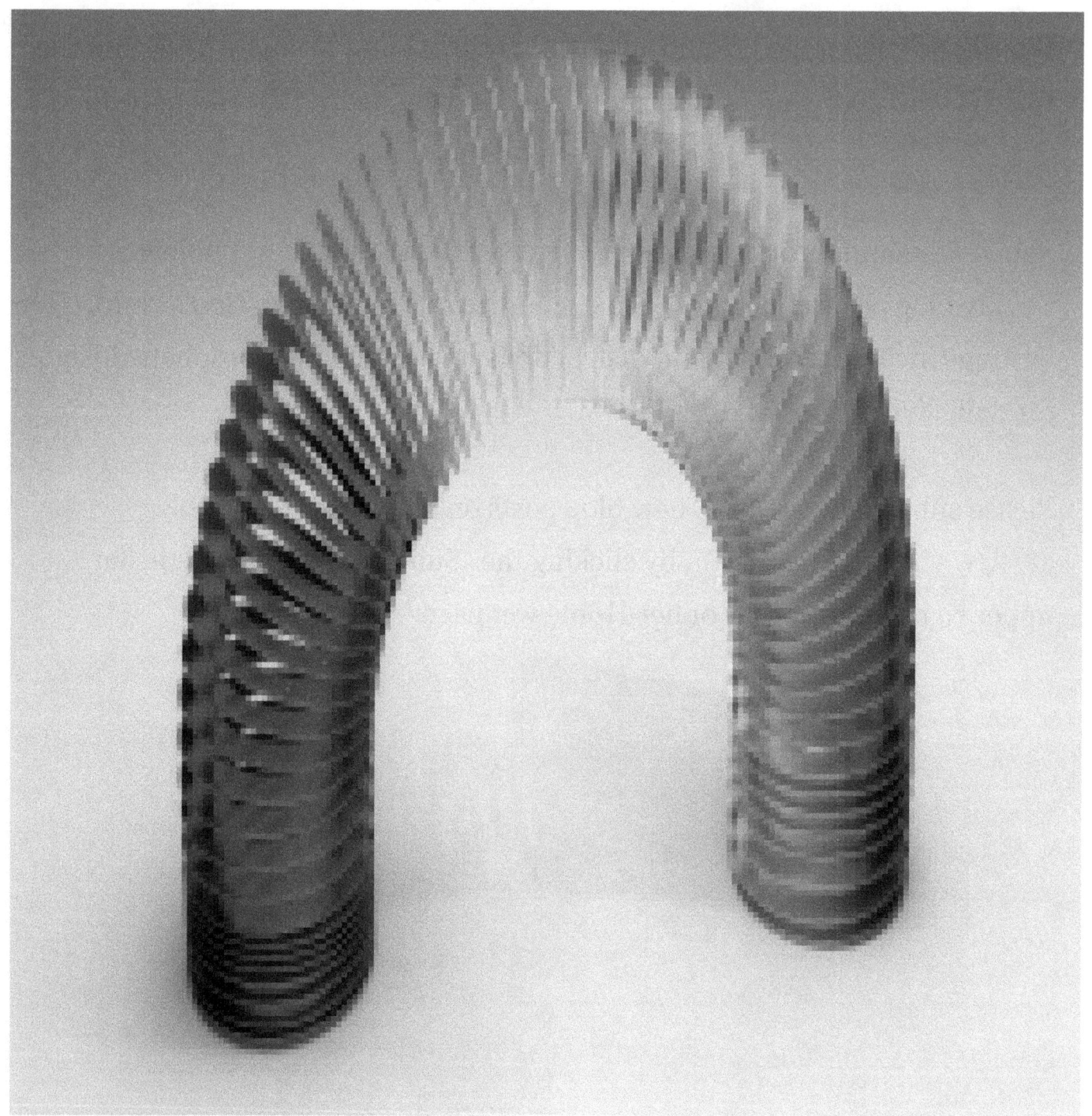

Blessed Are The Flexible

September 1, 2021
Encouragement

En route to our grandson's baptism last Sunday morning, I drove past a local business whose outside marquee read, "Life is all about how you handle Plan B." Upon reading this, my spirit was stirred and challenged. One of my "Sheilaisms" for the past few years has been, "Blessed are the flexible for they will never be bent out of shape!" While this may cause some to chuckle, it's much easier said than done, especially in dire situations when living life.

The "Plan B" words stuck in my spirit as rhetorical questions began to follow. What if this plan came and went, we're still searching, and are on about "Plan ZZZ" by this point in time? Then what?

Your Tallest Mountain

What's the biggest mountain or obstacle that you are facing now? Is it the loss of a loved one, an ongoing health challenge, a relationship issue, a court decision, financial pressure, or do you get the gist of my query?

_____
_____
_____

How long have you been facing this particular mountain or been trying to scale it to get to the top?

_____
_____

When you first encountered your challenge, did you have a "Plan B?" How many "plans" have you implemented since then if you're still waiting?

Psalm 46

When I encounter huge obstacles and tall, rugged mountains, I try to remember the words of Psalm 46:

"God *is* our refuge and strength,
A very present help in trouble.
Therefore we will not fear,
Even though the earth be removed,
And though the mountains be carried into the midst of the sea;
Though its waters roar *and* be troubled,
Though the mountains shake with its swelling. *Selah*
There is a river whose streams shall make glad the city of God,
The holy *place* of the tabernacle of the Most High.
God *is* in the midst of her, she shall not be moved;
God shall help her, just at the break of dawn.

The nations raged, the kingdoms were moved;

He uttered His voice, the earth melted.

The Lord of hosts *is* with us;

The God of Jacob *is* our refuge. *Selah*

Come, behold the works of the Lord,

Who has made desolations in the earth.

He makes wars cease to the end of the earth;

He breaks the bow and cuts the spear in two;

He burns the chariot in the fire.

Be still, and know that I *am* God;

I will be exalted among the nations,

I will be exalted in the earth!

The Lord of hosts *is* with us;

The God of Jacob *is* our refuge. *Selah*"

Verse 10a is so instructive and lends such comfort, "Be still, and know that I *am* God" even amid the equivalent of our problems being likened unto the earth moving under our feet, the waters roaring around us, and the mountains shaking. (Verses 2-3)

There's a reason that verse 7, "The LORD of hosts *is* with us; The God of Jacob *is* our refuge," is repeated in verse 11 at the end of this psalm. Psalm 23 is a great companion to Psalm 46.

Perhaps our natural inclination is to formulate our own "Plan B," but God's help and solutions are a much better choice even if we don't agree with them at the time.

During the time I began reciting my one-liner, "Blessed are the flexible for they will never be bent out of shape," I envisioned a large piece of elastic that could be stretched a great length.

When searching for images of elastic to accompany this week's blog post, I couldn't find exactly what I wanted, so I opted for a slinky since it's actually quite flexible. Also, I located a fun demonstration of how to use one. Here's the link if you'd like to watch it:

https://www.google.com/search?q=how+does+a+slinky+work&rlz=1C1CHBF_enUS800US801&oq=how+does+a+slinky+work&aqs=chrome..69i57j0i2i30l5j0i390l2.3015j0j7&sourceid=chrome&ie=UTF-8#kpvalbx=_bJcuYejzL8iT-AbuhamIAw29

<u>Prophetic Insights For Daily Living</u>

#1. What's your normal practice of living life when your plans suddenly change and not for the better?
_____
_____
_____

#2. Do you seek God first or start burning up your cell phone minutes seeking advice from others? There's absolutely nothing wrong with enlisting prayer support and Godly counsel. Our flesh can sometimes want to do this right away instead of waiting on the Lord for His direction.

_____
_____
_____
_____

#3. What would be your words of encouragement to those who are experiencing difficult times?

_____
_____
_____

#4. Is it a challenge for you to remain flexible when things go south in a hurry?

_____
_____
_____

#5. Psalm 9:9-10 are verses of assurance and comfort, "The Lord also will be a refuge for the oppressed, A refuge in times of trouble. And those who know Your name will put their trust in You; For You, Lord, have not forsaken those who seek You."

#6. Are there additional verses you could add to the ones above?

_____
_____
_____
_____

Speaking of living life, much of our world is currently in crisis and chaos. When writing this blog post, I'm most certainly not taking any of it lightly. As I reflect upon my drive to our annual "Church In The Park" followed by the opportunity to be baptized in the river, I realize that the local business could have listed anything on its marquee board. In my heart and spirit, I know God wanted me to see their message and read it.

One major aspect of adult life is how we handle it when things go sideways and/or the bottom falls out. Ergo, I'm trying to remember to recite my "Elastic One-Liner" when this happens. Or I just might purchase a glitzy slinky, watch the young man's online demonstration, and practice a few of his suggestions just for grins!

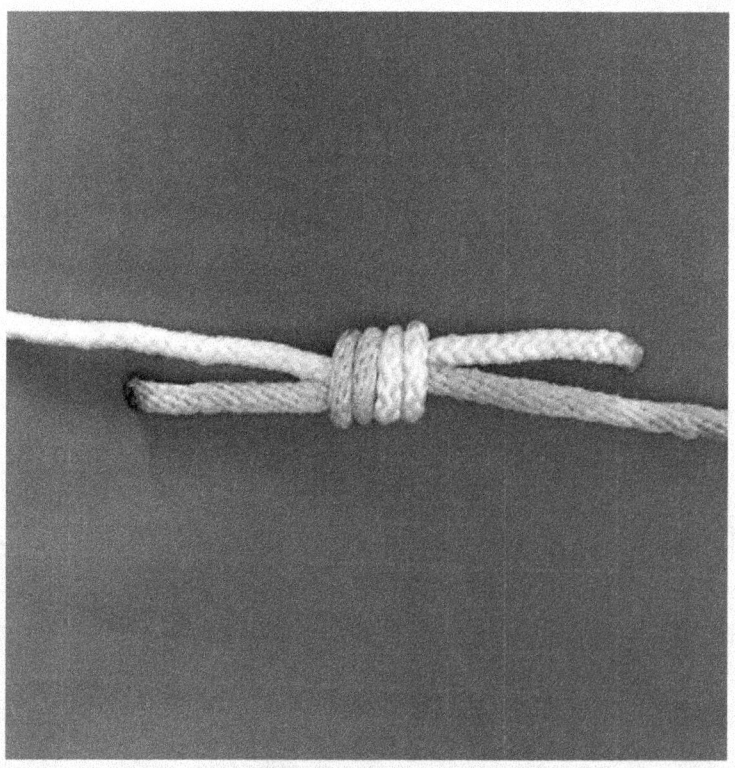

The Stubborn Knot Before You

https://sheilaeismann.com/lifes-challenges/

Brothers and sisters in our Lord Jesus, we can always trust our Heavenly Father to take care of us. God is good, and He always has a perfect plan for everything under the sun and in our lives.

"Enter into His gates with thanksgiving,
And into His courts with praise.
Be thankful to Him, and bless His name.
For the Lord is good;
His mercy is everlasting,
And His truth endures to all generations." (Psalm 100:4-5)

Sheila Eismann, Prophetic Seer, Blogger, Author & Teacher, publishes her weekly blog posts endeavoring to encourage others through God's word. Her writings include teaching and instructions on how to apply prophetic insights for daily living.

Please subscribe to receive new blog posts on her website at www.sheilaeismann.com by clicking the "Subscribe" button in the far upper right-hand corner of her Home webpage.

Sheila Eismann

Like A Tree Planted By The Waters

September 7, 2021
Encouragement

We can learn so much from nature and its cycles. In some of His parables, our Lord Jesus cited examples from everyday surroundings to convey Biblical truths. Much to my dismay, the leaves of our gorgeous silver maples are turning from dark green to bright red much earlier than normal. This is due primarily to the severe drought and above-average summer temperatures even though we live in the desert. When observing the delicate leaves gently falling to the ground, I was reminded of the verse from Jeremiah 17:8, "For he shall be like a tree planted by the waters."

God fully proclaimed through His prophet Jeremiah what woes were to befall Judah and its surrounding nations and the reasons for them. However, God also delivered hope and plans for a future restoration for His people. (Jeremiah 29:11)

In Jeremiah 17:5-6, our Lord cautions against trusting in man and departing from Him. A most encouraging contrast and promise are stated in verses 7-8:

"Blessed *is* the man who trusts in the LORD,
And whose hope is in the LORD.

For he shall be like a tree planted by the waters,

Which spreads out its roots by the river,

And will not fear when heat comes;

But its leaf will be green,

And will not be anxious in the year of drought,

Nor will cease from yielding fruit."

Trees, Rivers, Leaves & Fruit

As I was preparing this message, I sensed The Holy Spirit wanted us to pay close attention to each line of Jeremiah 17:7-8 and do a self-examination of sorts:

#1. Are we fully trusting in the Lord?

_____
_____
_____

#2. Do we have continued hope in Jesus despite what is going on in our chaotic world?

_____
_____
_____

If our answers to questions one and two above are "Yes," then we are likened unto a tree planted by the waters.

#3. A tree symbolizes a person, righteous believer, our life, the kingdom of God, family, Jesus, and the cross.

#4. Water is the life source for a tree just like it is for humans. Spiritually speaking, water is symbolic of The Holy Spirit Who is given to each one of us when we accept Jesus Christ as our Lord and Savior. (John 4:10-14, 7:38-39, 14:17; Acts 2:38, and Galatians 4:6)

#5. Once the tree is planted by a continual water source, it spreads out its roots by the river. Roots represent our heart and Jesus Christ Who is to be the foundation or taproot of our life.

#6. Rivers symbolize the river of life, The Holy Spirit or a move of The Holy Spirit, the Word of God, a boundary or border, eternity, and river of life. (Revelation 22:1)

#7. A tree that is planted by the waters will not fear when heat comes, will have green leaves, and will not be anxious in a year of drought. For a good contrast and word picture, please take a closer look at the image which accompanies this week's blog post. The tree directly behind the one whose leaves have already turned bright red is as green as grass. This one could be likened to a tree that is planted by the waters.

I like the following quote from Donald Miller,

"All the trees are losing their leaves, and not one of them is worried."

The Apostle Paul penned the following verses while under house arrest in Rome,

"Be anxious for nothing, but in everything by prayer and supplication, with thanksgiving, let your requests be made known to God; and the peace of God, which surpasses all understanding, will guard your hearts and minds through Christ Jesus." (Philippians 4:6-7)

#8. This tree continues to bear fruit. One of the symbolisms for roots is the foundation without which no fruit can be grown.

So, we can see the **progression** stated in Jeremiah 17:7-8 for how to continue to bear fruit in our lives.

(a)Trust in the Lord.
(b)Hope in the Lord.
(c)Spread out our roots by the river of life (by way of The Holy Spirit and the word of God).
(d)The only fear we're to have is the holy, reverential fear of God. Fear of man is a trap and a snare. (Proverbs 29:25)
(e)Be anxious for nothing. Anxiety is a lack of trust in God. Jesus addresses this in Matthew 6:25-34. If you find yourself becoming anxious, what can you do to increase your faith, hope, and trust in God? Recall the former times in which He has helped you, read His word, pray, praise Him in worship, take communion, and rest in Him.
(f)Co-labor with The Holy Spirit to continue to bear fruit. (Galatians 5:22-23)

Different Types of Droughts

Broadly speaking for a spiritual application, there can be different types of droughts, if you will, such as:

Financial

Health

Employment

Relationships

Familial

Spiritual

What other "droughts" would you add to this ongoing list?

_____

_____

The Supernatural Hope Flower

Throughout this long, hot, smoky summer, I wrote blog posts describing petals of a yellow, supernatural "Hope Flower." These were a series of prophetic visions I received which added a petal each week to complete the floral picture. You can read each one of them on my website www.sheilaeismann.com. Here's the message from Petal #8.

Supernatural Hope Flower

https://sheilaeismann.com/exercise-your-faith/

Prophetic Insights For Daily Living

#1. A good companion study for this week's blog post is John 15. While this might seem to negate the positive aspect of my message from Jeremiah 17:7-8, Jesus's instructions regarding bearing fruit are vital.

#2. Are you experiencing a spiritual drought? If so, what practical and spiritual steps have you taken that have helped you? If needed, revisit the **progression** from Jeremiah 17:7-8 regarding bearing fruit.

_____
_____
_____
_____

#3. God assigned His prophet Jeremiah to Judah and Jerusalem to warn them and the surrounding nations of what was going to happen to them because of sin and idolatry. Also, God gave Jeremiah messages of hope and restoration to be delivered as well. Those who heeded God's words through Jeremiah and went to Babylon willingly instead of intentionally defecting to Egypt fared far better. Egypt symbolizes the world.

#4. Perhaps some of those living in Babylon viewed their lives as a "drought" for the entire 70 years they resided there (Jeremiah 29:10), but God still had a plan and provided for them during their captivity. Do you feel like you've lived in a drought at some time in the past? How did God provide for you, and how did He lead you during that time?

_____
_____
_____
_____

#5. The present-day challenge may be somewhat the same for us in that we may not be real happy campers with God's provision or our place of habitation (Acts 17:26). Those of us in the west are still literally living in a smoke-filled drought with virtually dry water reservoirs and loss of income and all that encompasses due to diminished water supplies.

https://www.reuters.com/world/us/us-declares-first-ever-shortage-western-reservoir-triggering-water-cuts-2021-08-16/

I want to encourage all of us to continue to trust God and place our hope in Him, His Son, Jesus Christ, and The Holy Spirit. They always have our best interest at heart and a plan for hope and restoration.

"Let us therefore come boldly to the throne of grace, that we may obtain mercy and find grace to help in time of need." (Hebrews 4:16)

Sheila Eismann, Prophetic Seer, Blogger, Author & Teacher, publishes her weekly blog posts endeavoring to encourage others through God's word. Her writings include teaching and instructions on how to apply prophetic insights for daily living.

Please subscribe to receive new blog posts on her website at www.sheilaeismann.com by clicking the "Subscribe" button in the far upper right-hand corner of her Home webpage.

Prophetic Insights For Daily Living – Volume 3

The Woman and The Candle

September 13, 2021
Prophetic Visions

During the late afternoon of September 5, 2021, the last day of the Hebrew year 5781, I saw a woman in the Spirit holding a white saucer. There was a small stub of a white candle burning in the center of it. I was a bit perplexed, so I continued to wait on the Lord and pray into this prophetic vision of the woman and the candle as her light was about to go out. On the eve of the Feast of Trumpets ushering in the new Jewish year 5782, September 6th, I saw the last few flickers of the flame on the candle resting on the saucer. I wondered if it would be lights out!

In the next scene of the prophetic vision, the woman was given a new candle that was burning brightly. When it was handed to her, she seemed so relieved and overcome with joy.

End of vision.

The Hebrew Year 5781

The Hebrew letters and pictures (ancient and modern) for 5781 were Pey which symbolizes mouth, voice, and open. It was a "Double Pey," so to speak, as it was not only the year of Pey but the first year in the decade of Pey.

It's beyond ironic and sad that in a double Pey year, so many mouths had to be covered with masks and voices could not be heard because of a worldwide pestilence.

The Hebrew Year 5782

We're now entering the Hebrew year of Bet which is the second year in the Pey decade. The Hebrew letters and pictures for Bet (ancient and modern) represent a house, family, and inside.

Let Your Light Shine

Jesus drew His disciples to Him on the Mount of Olives and gave this instruction to them among many others,

"You are the light of the world. A city that is set on a hill cannot be hidden. Nor do they light a lamp and put it under a basket, but on a lampstand, and it gives light to all *who are* in the house. Let your light so shine before men, that they may see your good works and glorify your Father in heaven." (Matthew 5:14-16)

A candle is symbolic of light, a believer in Jesus Christ, the spirit of a man, the Spirit of God, the Word of God, and the church.

The candle in the vision could have been any color, but it appeared as a bright, white one that represents light, purity, righteousness, and holiness.

Instead of being in a candleholder, the candle was sitting on a saucer. The plate is representative of food, provision, resources and supply, portion and/or serving, a person's heart, motive or agenda, or giving someone what they deserve.

Lights Out

A diminishing candle or one that is about to burn out represents losing or turning from Jesus Christ, our first love.

To each of the 7 churches mentioned in the first part of the Book of Revelation, there is a message sent by Jesus to the messenger of each one of them. They are commended for their good works or deeds but warned about their shortcomings (except for the churches at Smyrna and Philadelphia) and advised what corrections need to be made post-haste.

There's a stern warning to the church of Ephesus, "Nevertheless I have *this* against you, that you have left your first love." (Revelation 2:4) Jesus Christ was no longer their first love.

Bright Lights

Light has many meanings, some of which are: your life, a righteous life or heart, Jesus Christ as He is the light of the world (John 8:12), revelation, God's word as a light unto our path (Psalm 119:105), fellowship as walking in the light (1 John 1:7), and the true Christian church where the real Jesus Christ is taught and not a counterfeit. The modern-day cults have their own version of Jesus.

Inside Your House & Family

My husband and I enjoy candlelight dinners, especially during the winter evenings since the days are so short. We procured some made from beeswax which is wonderful for those of us who unfortunately have allergic reactions to some candles. These particular candles are slow-burning and give off a lot of light. They come in different shapes and sizes, so I've placed them at various spots throughout our house.

As I've prayed into the interpretation of this vision, one explanation could be that the woman's spirit has been renewed, so she can let her light shine inside her house for her family.

"For You will light my lamp. The LORD my God will enlighten my darkness." (Psalm 18:28)

This would combine all three major components of the ancient and modern pictures for Bet which are house, family, and inside.

A Year of Invitations

The Spirit of the Lord is impressing upon me this will be a year to invite not only your family but those who need to come into the family of God to candlelight dinners. If all of us will step out of our comfort zones and follow the leading of The Holy Spirit, many will be drawn to the one and only true light, Jesus Christ. As you testify about what He has done for you and your family, the flame of your candle will greatly expand in length and proximity.

Kindness Is Spiritual Currency

https://sheilaeismann.com/spiritual-currency/

Perhaps you are a person who lives alone with limited means or has a flock of kids and there's no budget for a candle. God will provide just what you need when you need it. This is part of the joy of walking in faith and victory!

The Parable Of The Lost Coin

"Or what woman, having ten silver coins, if she loses one coin, does not light a lamp, sweep the house, and search carefully until she finds *it?* And when she has found *it,* she calls *her* friends and neighbors together, saying, 'Rejoice with me, for I have found the piece which I lost!' Likewise, I say to you, there is joy in the presence of the angels of God over one sinner who repents."
(Luke 15:8-10)

Prophetic Insights For Daily Living

#1. How does this prophetic vision speak to you?

_____
_____
_____
_____

#2. Can you relate to the woman whose candle was on its last flicker only to be revived by our Lord Jesus and given new opportunities and assignments? If your light is about to go out, what can you do to get a new one?

_____
_____
_____
_____

#3. If you are led to purchase some extra candles, to whom would you gift them?

_____
_____
_____
_____

#4. Who would you invite to a candlelight dinner inside your home?

_____
_____
_____
_____

#5. I would highly encourage you to start a prophetic journal for the Hebrew year 5782 to record how God will empower you to let your light shine. Mark your calendar for September 26, 2022, the start of the new Jewish year 5783 to review what you've written during the previous year. Prepare to be amazed!

#6. Don't allow discouragement to set in. Even if you're the only light in your family, school, place of employment, or neighborhood, you can make a significant difference. Jesus is the light of the world, and He is with you every hour of every day. Many tried unsuccessfully to extinguish His light before His appointed time but were unable to do so.

#7. This is an anointed and appointed year to draw closer to God, purify our lives with His help and comfort, and let our light shine ever so brightly! (James 4:8 and 1 Peter 1:15-16)

#8. Pray and ask God what He wants to do inside your house and family during 5782.

_____
_____
_____
_____
_____
_____

This verse is for someone out there in blogger-reader land:

"Therefore do not cast away your confidence, which has great reward." (Hebrews 10:35)

I would like to bless you with a little of my free-flowing verse ~~

L I G H T

L – Love is a priceless gift

I – Intended for all mankind

G – Given by God above

H – Help to spread it far and wide

T – 'Til the end of time.

"Blessed are those who have learned to acclaim you, who walk in the light of your presence, Lord." (Psalm 89:15 NIV)

Sheila Eismann, Prophetic Seer, Blogger, Author & Teacher, publishes her weekly blog posts endeavoring to encourage others through God's word. Her writings include teaching and instructions on how to apply prophetic insights for daily living.

Please subscribe to receive new blog posts on her website at www.sheilaeismann.com by clicking the "Subscribe" button in the far upper right-hand corner of her Home webpage.

Sheila Eismann

Your Rest Will Be Your Reset

September 21, 2021
Prophetic Words

While spending time with the Lord on September 16, 2021, in reading His word, prayer, and worshipping Him, I heard the following in the Spirit, "Your rest will be your reset." This occurred during Yom Kippur, the Day of Atonement. It's important to understand that while we are no longer under the law but under grace (Romans 10:4), we need to appreciate that atonement for our sins came through Jesus's death on the cross. 1 John 1:9 reassures us that, "If we confess our sins, He is faithful and just to forgive us *our* sins and to cleanse us from all unrighteousness."

This prophetic word, "Your Rest Will Be Your Reset," is encouragement for the weary. Envision yourself sitting by the still waters as you read this week's blog post.

Next, I received a prophetic vision wherein I saw someone standing in a completely dried-out pasture. There wasn't a sign of green vegetation anywhere. Since I was raised on a farm, the Lord will oftentimes speak to me via agricultural terms or pictures. I heard an invitation in the Spirit, "Come into the lush green pasture that has a secure fence around it."

In the next scene of the vision, I saw a new, human heart. I heard in the Spirit, "A fresh heart will give you a new restart."

Rest, Reset, Restart, Renewal & Reassurance

#1. Rest

In the Old Testament, after Israel left Egypt and headed toward the promised land, they were required to rest at various intervals in the desert. God decided when they were to rest and when they were to be on the move. He did this through the cloud of His glory.

"Whenever the cloud was taken up from above the tabernacle, the children of Israel would go onward in all their journeys. But if the cloud was not taken up, then they did not journey till the day that it was taken up. For the cloud of the Lord *was* above the tabernacle by day, and the fire was over it by night, in the sight of all the house of Israel, throughout all their journeys." (Exodus 40:36-38)

Genesis 2:1-3 informs us that God rested on the 7th day of His creation foreshadowing how to keep the Sabbath day holy.

In the New Testament, we're under grace, so we don't necessarily have to adhere to the strict Old Testament rules and regulations about keeping the Sabbath Day exclusively. Our Sabbath doesn't necessarily need to be on Sunday. We have the luxury and invitation to rest with Jesus Christ our Lord any time on any given day.

Jesus rested on different days at different times during His earthly ministry. And, if there was ever anyone Who needed rest, it was Him due to the sheer demands upon His life and ministry.

After Jesus sent out His twelve disciples who preached, cast out demons, anointed many with oil who were sick, and healed them ((Mark 6:12), they gathered to Him and told Jesus what they had done and taught. His response was, "Come aside by yourselves to a deserted place and rest awhile." (Mark 6:31) In the disciples' rest was their reset to go back into the highways and byways to advance the kingdom of God among them.

Are you in need of rest?

_____
_____
_____

#2. Reset

At the advent of the worldwide pandemic, **_reset_** became quite the buzzword regarding a reset of world governments, economies, institutions, regulations, practices, and on rolls the proverbial Reset River. Despite what imposed effects and results all of this will happen to be as we progress through the end of 2021 and into 2022, our omnipotent, omniscient, and omnipresent God has His own type of reset in Him. This comes through His Son, Jesus Christ, who spoke these words in Matthew 11:28-30, "Come to Me, all *you* who labor and are heavily laden, and I will give you rest. Take My yoke upon you and learn from Me, for I am gentle and lowly in heart, and you will find rest for your souls. For My yoke *is* easy and My burden is light."

Contextually speaking from the above-referenced verses in the book of Matthew, Jesus was describing the Jews who were suffering under a heavy load of religiously dictated responsibilities laid on them by the Pharisees, rabbis, scribes, and priests of their day. The **rest** Jesus spoke of meant relief from these unrealistic and burdensome tasks and way of life. The Greek word for rest is *anapauo,* Strong's G373 which has three basic meanings:

"I. to cause or permit one to cease from any movement or labour in order to recover and collect his strength;

II. to give rest, refresh, to give one's self rest, take rest;

III. to keep quiet, of calm and patient expectation."

https://www.blueletterbible.org/lexicon/g373/kjv/tr/0-1/

In John 8:31-35, Jesus addressed those Jews who made the correct choice and believed in Him. He reassured them in verse 36, "Therefore if the Son makes you free, you shall be free indeed."

"Jesus Christ *is* the same yesterday, today, and forever." (Hebrews 13:8) His invitation still stands to everyone on the planet today. It's as if time has stood still concerning this.

Suffice it to say, a spiritual reset will help us to navigate the imposed, physical resets in our lives.

Is there anything in your life that needs reset?

#3. Restart

"A fresh heart will give you a new restart." Through the daily grind even absent a worldwide pandemic, our hearts can get weighed down with many things.

King Solomon, the wisest man who ever lived, other than Jesus Christ, gave this sage advice, "Above all else, guard your heart, for everything you do flows from it." (Proverbs 4:23 NIV) Considering all the king had going on in his life, he most certainly wrote this from wisdom's lofty vantage point.

Borrowing King David's poignant words in Psalm 51:10, "Create in me a clean heart, O God, And renew a steadfast spirit within me." He continues in verse 17, "The sacrifices of God *are* a broken spirit, A broken and a contrite heart—These, O God, You will not despise."

Psalm 139:23-24 starts the restart:

"Search me, O God, and know my heart;
Try me, and know my anxieties;
And see if *there is any* wicked way in me,
And lead me in the way everlasting."

This calls for vigilance on our part and a yielding to allow God to search our hearts to show us if there's any evil in it. Daily Bible reading helps us to be "washed with the water of the word." (Ephesians 5:26) "For the word of God is alive and active. Sharper than any double-edged sword, it penetrates even to dividing soul and spirit, joints and marrow; it judges the thoughts and attitudes of the heart." (Hebrews 4:12 NIV)

There's the mention of God promising a new, undivided heart to the Israelites in Ezekiel 11:20. The result of this will be obedience to the commandments of God. The fulfillment of this prophecy will occur during the millennial reign of Christ when Israel is restored to faith. (Romans 11:26)

For New Testament believers, our hearts were transformed when we accepted Jesus Christ as our personal Lord and Savior. (Romans 10:9-10) Keeping them in a fresh state of renewal will definitely aid with a restart in applicable areas of our lives and spiritual walk.

Sometimes, things need to be reset before they can be restarted.

_____
_____
_____

#4. Renewal

Is there anything that you need renewing in your life today? If so, what is it? Have you tried doing it in your own strength? How's that working for you?

___

___

___

Joshua renewed the covenant with Israel by reading all the words of the law, including the blessings and the curses. (Joshua 8:30-35)

When we wait on the Lord and rest in Him, our strength is renewed.

"Even the youths shall faint and be weary,
And the young men shall utterly fall,
But those who wait on the Lord
Shall renew *their* strength;
They shall mount up with wings like eagles,
They shall run and not be weary,
They shall walk and not faint." (Isaiah 40:30-31)
Isaiah 30:15, "In quietness and confidence is your strength."

The more the world spins out of control, the less we are to be conformed to it. We are transformed by the renewing of our minds. (Romans 12:2)

Earlier this year, I wrote a blog post regarding waiting upon the Lord. Here's the link for it if you'd like to read and revisit it.

https://sheilaeismann.com/freedom-from-anxiety/

#5. Reassurance

The completely dried out pasture in this prophetic vision followed by the lush green pasture invitation reminds us of the comforting psalm of King David portraying the Lord, the Shepherd of His people. There's so much reassurance in the 6 verses of Psalm 23. It's one my husband and I've chosen to memorize and pray aloud on our daily walks.

If we contrast the two pastures to the verses, it would be as if none of the benefits of Psalm 23 were present until the woman chose to enter the new pasture with the secure gate. John Chapter 10 highlights Jesus as the good and true shepherd Who knows His sheep, and He is the gate or door for them.

The symbolism for pasture is ultra-obvious which is a feeding ground; however, what we eat will manifest in many areas of our lives.

The present reality and state of our nation and world demand a reassurance of Jesus's presence in all that we are and do. Many of the old church hymns were borne as a result of the trials and tribulations of saints who have already graduated to heaven and are among the great cloud of witnesses. (Hebrews 12:1) They most probably drew strength and inspiration from reassurance in Jesus while they walked the earth.

Prophetic Insights For Daily Living

#1. Which of the 5 "R's" speak to you the loudest, i.e., rest, reset, restart, renewal or reassurance? Or perhaps there's more than one that stirred your spirit.

#2. Do you find it difficult to carve out time to rest amidst your daily schedule?

#3. Rest can come in many different forms. It doesn't always have to be reclining in a chair or sleeping in a bed. Some examples would be: cease from striving with anyone or anything; turning off a constant news feed; or saying no to things we know we don't have time to do or that God has not assigned us to complete.

#4. What are your "rest thieves" that rob you consistently or from time to time?

#5. Do you feel you need a reset in any area of your spiritual or physical life?

#6. I deem this prophetic word is not only encouragement for the weary, but all of us as we embark upon the new Hebraic year 5782.

Fellow saints, rest in God, so He can reset whatever you need!

Sheila Eismann, Prophetic Seer, Blogger, Author & Teacher, publishes her weekly blog posts endeavoring to encourage others through God's word. Her writings include teaching and instructions on how to apply prophetic insights for daily living.

Please subscribe to receive new blog posts on her website at www.sheilaeismann.com by clicking the "Subscribe" button in the far upper right-hand corner of her Home webpage.

4 Keys To Open 4 Doors

September 28, 2021
Prophetic Visions

During the time of praise and worship of our local church on Sunday, September 26, 2021, the Spirit realm opened, and I saw 4 keys to open 4 doors. A person was sitting at a workbench in a craft studio setting. A wooden box of small bottles of paint such as one would use for model airplanes or cars was sitting to her right. She'd been painting four keys with several coats of gold-colored paint. The keys featured in this blog post aren't gold; however, they resemble what I saw in this prophetic vision. As I waited before the Lord, He continued to point me toward the importance of spiritual gold.

Scene #2

4 doors appeared in the Spirit which the woman had tried repeatedly to open but could not do so. As one would look from left to right at a set of 4 doors in front of them, the sign on each appeared as follows:

LOVE
KINDNESS
GOODNESS
GENTLENESS

Scene #3

As the woman fingered the individual bottles inside the wooden box, she picked up a bottle of paint remover. After cleaning and polishing the keys, she tried to open the locked doors and was finally successful!

The sense I had is these doors pertain to the area of relationships, especially re-establishing and strengthening them.

Just like the woman in the Spirit was painting the keys with several layers of gold paint, the onset of a worldwide pandemic has added "extra layers" to an already divided country. Places and people are becoming more locked out and locked down than ever before. This pertains to not only familial relationships, but those in our neighborhoods, schools, workplaces, churches, and so forth.

Each coat of paint that was applied is equivalent to the woman trying to navigate relationships in her own strength.

After the extra coats of paint were removed and the keys were cleaned, the woman could open the doors easily.

Walking in the flesh vs. walking in the Spirit.

Walking and operating in the flesh will not open the doors that need to be opened. These four particular fruits of the Spirit listed in Galatians 5:22-23 are empowered by The Holy Spirit to produce the necessary fruit to re-open, strengthen and increase relationships:

LOVE
KINDNESS
GOODNESS
GENTLENESS

These 4 keys are not necessarily sequential. As you read, study, and pray into this prophetic word, The Holy Spirit will show you which of these keys and doors He wants you to pursue first. For example, if love is number one and you're desiring to have that door opened, God may show you that peace must first be established in the relationship before it can be restored. You can't move forward until there's peace.

There was much division in the church in Galatia which caused the Apostle Paul to admonish them accordingly, "I say then: Walk in the Spirit, and you shall not fulfill the lust of the flesh. For the flesh lusts against the Spirit, and the Spirit against the flesh; and these are contrary to one another, so that you do not do the things that you wish. But if you are led by the Spirit, you are not under the law." (Galatians 5:16-18)

The layers of paint the woman used to cover the keys made them too thick to fit into the keyhole. These layers are likened to the layers of the flesh. Once the flesh is removed revealing the pure gold, the doors could be opened. Walking in the Spirit will open the doors.

How do you walk in the Spirit? Submit your flesh along with its desires and ways to God. Study the word of God, choose to submit to it, and walk it out.

This set of keys bears your name.

God's supreme wisdom via His specific strategies is not a one-size-fits-all for everyone. There will be fundamental, basic ways in which to express genuine love, kindness, goodness, and gentleness. However, if someone or a group of people such as co-workers push back against what you're trying to accomplish, inherent within your individual God-anointed key will contain what you need to open the door. This set of keys bears your name, so you will be the one to unlock the door.

You'll have to spend time with Jesus. He will download a definite strategy and the timing to implement it. Record what He shows you to do along with the accompanying scriptures from your Bible. Prophetic journaling is a splendid method for recording your God-given strategies and assignments.

Studying the symbolism.

#1. The number 4 represents worldwide, universal, creation, the spirit realm (the 4th dimension), rule or dominion, or an open door (Revelation 4:1).

#2. Keys are symbolic of the gifts of the Spirit, signs and wonders, authority, access, a way out of something, God's will, prayer, opportunities, revelation, prophecy, knowledge, wisdom, heart, the main or "key" person, and love.

#3. Gold portrays kingship, royalty, honor, kingdom glory, God, authority, man-made gods, deeds performed via someone by and through the power of The Holy Spirit, wealth, first place (Olympics), blessings, valuable, and gold refined in the fire (Revelation 3:18).

#4. Paint or painted used in the verb form (the woman was painting with gold paint in the prophetic vision) speaks of cover-up or putting on a show of some sort of adornment or preparation.

The noun form of paint portrays an illustration or image, the representation or likeness of someone or something, an idol, view of something, or covering something with color.

#5. Doors symbolize Jesus Christ (Revelation 3:20); decisions (there were 4 doors in this prophetic vision); entrance, heart, faith, mouth, and opportunities.

The battle began in the garden.

The battle over relationships began in the Garden of Eden and hasn't stopped since. As long as there's an enemy of our souls who's still on the loose causing division and strife until he's thrown into the bottomless pit (Revelation 20:1-3), we must always follow Jesus Christ, our Lord, and Savior, and obey His word.

What you eat will open the doors.

It's instructive to revisit the first 3 chapters of Genesis from time to time. Eve ate of the forbidden fruit in the Garden of Eden, and mankind has paid the heavy price ever since that day.

Now here's a pair of 4's for you from Matthew 4:4:

"But He (Jesus) answered (the devil) and said, "It is written, 'Man shall not live by bread alone, but by every word that proceeds from the mouth of God.'"

Considering the 4 doors which appeared in this prophetic vision, let's say for illustrative purposes that The Holy Spirit has shown you that the first door He wants to help you open is **KINDNESS.** Commence with a few verses regarding kindness and chew slowly on them spiritually speaking just like you would enjoy a dish of raspberry sorbet or whatever would be considered your special treat.

Here are a couple of scriptures to help jumpstart your project:

"And be kind to one another, tenderhearted, forgiving one another, even as God in Christ forgave you." (Ephesians 4:32)

"For you, brethren, have been called to liberty; only do not *use* liberty as an opportunity for the flesh, but through love serve one another." (Galatians 5:13)

"Or do you show contempt for the riches of his kindness, forbearance and patience, not realizing that God's kindness is intended to lead you to repentance?" (Romans 2:4, NIV)

As you slowly digest your spiritual food, it will manifest in the natural.

Keep your eyes peeled as it will surely come to pass!

https://sheilaeismann.com/spiritual-currency/

Kindness is Spiritual Currency

This most likely will not be a "Eureka Overnight" experience since it takes time to grow fruit. Wounded people may not readily accept kindness. They have to first learn to trust. As you walk with God and learn to trust Him, He will give you His anointed strategy to show genuine kindness to someone to repair a relationship.

"For My thoughts *are* not your thoughts,
Nor *are* your ways My ways," says the Lord.
"For *as* the heavens are higher than the earth,
So are My ways higher than your ways,
And My thoughts than your thoughts." (Isaiah 55:8-9)

Prophetic Insights For Daily Living:

#1. The woman painted the keys with gold paint which is covering the truth of whatever the situation is with fake gold color. After the false appearance is removed, the truth can be found, one can face it, and walk through open doors.

#2. For your most challenging relationship, whether personal or otherwise, God may show you the person's particular love language. As you implement this with His guidance and The Holy Spirit's fruit of love, kindness, goodness, and gentleness, watch those doors fly wide open!

#3. Enter the joy of following Jesus since He knows what it's going to take to open the doors. This can become a treasure hunt to us as we exercise our childlike faith in Him.

#4. Which of the four doors do you sense God wants to help you open first?

_____
_____
_____
_____

#5. What layers of paint (fleshly acts, patterns, or habits) do you need to remove such as the woman in the prophetic vision removed the layers of paint with paint remover?

_____
_____
_____
_____

#6. What's the equivalent of the paint: pride, unforgiveness, anger, lack of trust, jealousy, prejudice, spite, hate, or an unteachable spirit, etc.?

_____
_____

#7. As you study the prophetic symbolisms outlined in the blog post, what spiritual connections can you make between them?

#8. Just as an athlete physically trains to win the gold medal in the Olympics, we can become spiritual athletes who train for the spiritual gold.

With the sharp increase of Covid cases and uncertainty throughout the nations, may all of us make every effort to strengthen relationships. God, Jesus, and The Holy Spirit will help us as we co-labor with Them.

"If it is possible, as far as it depends on you, live at peace with everyone." (Romans 12:18, NIV)

Sheila Eismann, Prophetic Seer, Blogger, Author & Teacher, publishes her weekly blog posts endeavoring to encourage others through God's word. Her writings include teaching and instructions on how to apply prophetic insights for daily living.

Please subscribe to receive new blog posts on her website at www.sheilaeismann.com by clicking the "Subscribe" button in the far upper right-hand corner of her Home webpage.

Light, Grace & The Yellow Roses

October 5, 2021
Encouragement

One sunny afternoon 24 years ago during the merry month of May, our doorbell rang loudly. When I opened our front door, to my sheer delight there stood our precious grandkiddos, Aaron and Hannah. Along with their sweet mamma, the three of them came bearing my Mother's Day gift. Two-year-old Hannah was just as pleased as she could be while handing me a miniature yellow rose bush nestled inside a dark green, plastic holder. Aaron, her three-year-old brother, and Hannah had hand-selected this for me. Perhaps our beautiful daughter, Cathie, had steered them toward my all-time favorite flower when selecting such a thoughtful gift. The epiphany of light, grace, and the yellow roses just happened to come together this weekend. I think God in His goodness plants and plans serendipity along life's paths just for us, don't you?

_____

_____

_____

When I looked at the two, bright yellow roses in my herb garden late Friday afternoon, they reminded me of looking into the bright eyes of our older set of grandkiddos all those years ago. It was as if the two, miniature yellow roses were saying, "Hi, Grandma!" which made my heart smile.

Light & Grace

I felt stirred by The Holy Spirit to consult the meanings of our grandkiddos' names.

Aaron means "bringer of light." Psalm 27:1 accompanies his name, "The Lord *is* my light and my salvation; Whom shall I fear? The Lord *is* the strength of my life; Of whom shall I be afraid?"

The name Hannah exudes "grace and full of grace." The suggested lifetime scripture verse for her name is Psalm 84:11, "For the Lord God *is* a sun and shield; The Lord will give grace and glory; No good *thing* will He withhold From those who walk uprightly."

Flowers, Roses & The Color Yellow

(A) Flowers symbolize glory, prosperity, joy, the offering of praise to Jesus, life in and of itself, the upright in heart, and clothing.

(B) And what woman doesn't love roses which speak of love, beauty, Jesus Christ (the Rose of Sharon – Song of Solomon 2:1), and the church?

_____
_____
_____
_____

According to our daughter, Cathie, who's also a very talented free-lance artist, yellow roses represent friendship. Cathie spent innumerable hours illustrating her beautiful book titled, *Victorian Flora – Language of Flowers Handbook*. I enjoy just sitting down and looking through the beautiful artwork and all of the history and background for each of the flowers. I've even used it in dream interpretation and decoding of prophetic visions.

https://www.amazon.com/Victorian-Flora-Language-Flowers-Handbook-ebook/dp/B0848PS4N6/ref=sr_1_1?dchild=1&keywords=victorian+floral+by+cathie+richardson&qid=1633289022&sr=8-1

(C) The color yellow represents welcoming (think of the yellow ribbons tied around trees as America waited for her soldiers to return from the various wars in which we've been engaged over the centuries), friendship, and the glory of God.

During my younger years, yellow was near the bottom of my favorite color list. However, I'm discovering as I continue to walk with Jesus that the soft, buttercup yellow color really ministers to my soul and spirit. Do you happen to like the color yellow? When kitchen wallpaper was the rage, it was not uncommon to have a combination of yellow and blue as it represents the opposite spectrum of the color wheel and is most soothing to the eyes.

Resilient Roses & Weathering Life's Storms

In real life, this little rosebush is thriving like never before! It's weathered two major transplants, numerous disease infestations along with severe winters and cold weather. In fact, during some previous winters, we've lost other rose bushes, but this little, hearty one is still with us, thankfully.

Prophetic Insights For Daily Living

#1. God's grace (drawing upon the meaning of the name Hannah) helps us to weather the storms in our lives that don't necessarily arrive during the stormy weather seasons. Can you think of a time when He has helped you through one or more of them? God, Jesus, and The Holy Spirit are faithful even during the severest storm.

_____
_____
_____
_____

#2. Continuing with the theme of Hannah, full of grace, in which areas of your life do you need more grace? What's your favorite scripture pertaining to grace? At the top of my list is Ephesians 2:8-9, "For by grace you have been saved through faith, and that not of yourselves; *it is* the gift of God, not of works, lest anyone should boast."

_____
_____
_____
_____

True Christianity and Bible-believing and teaching churches add no works to salvation itself as this came through Jesus Christ, our Lord, and Savior, and Him alone. The cults mandate works to their man-made methods of salvation. Yes, faith without works is dead, (James 2:14-17), but this is entirely different than adding some type of works for man to be saved. Our good works in God's kingdom follow after we have accepted Jesus Christ as our Lord and Savior (Romans 10:9-10). It's by grace that we have been saved.

#3. Aaron, the bringer of light, adds life, strength, salvation, and lack of fear in our walk with Jesus. Do you have fear other than the holy, reverential fear of God in your life? If so, what is causing it? Have you been able to discern the root of it? Fear brings torment, but perfect love casts out fear. (1 John 4:18)

_____
_____
_____
_____

http://sheilaeismann.com/dream-therapy/

Flowers Send Their Own Invitations

God's creation is beyond amazing! Flowers send their own invitations to look at them, smell them, enjoy them, compare them, send them, decorate with them, and celebrate with them. The attributes of God are also reflected in the meanings of flowers such as love, friendship, guidance, reflection, prayer, reliance, justice, mercy, longsuffering, and many others.

What is your favorite flower, and what message is God sending you through it?

_____

_____

_____

_____

Have you experienced God's manner of serendipity in the past? Did it help to bolster your faith in Him and appreciation for Him?

_____

_____

_____

_____

The decade of the 70s is known for lots of things including plastic flowers and colored water. Some décor included a vase filled with this combination along with harvest orange and sage green hues of appliances, carpets, drapes, wall paint, and so forth throughout a house or apartment. That may sound ghastly now, but some women decorated their homes accordingly during this time frame.

If you live in an area that doesn't tolerate rose bushes very well or they're not your preference, perhaps you could round up a plastic yellow rose or a photo of one. Granted, you wouldn't be able to stop and smell the roses, but it could serve as a loving, friendly reminder of God's light and grace shed down upon you every day.

Sheila Eismann, Prophetic Seer, Blogger, Author & Teacher, publishes her weekly blog posts endeavoring to encourage others through God's word. Her writings include teaching and instructions on how to apply prophetic insights for daily living.

Please subscribe to receive new blog posts on her website at www.sheilaeismann.com. by clicking the "Subscribe" button in the far upper right-hand corner of her Home webpage.

Supernatural Sights & Sounds

October 14, 2021
Prophetic Teachings

Have you ever experienced the sound of a doorbell ringing when you were sound asleep but it did not ring in real life? Such was the case recently at 4:06 a.m. I've grown accustomed to hearing the unique sound of our ring doorbell system when someone presses it, but the one in the early morning hours of October 11, 2021, didn't sound like it. Later that morning, I checked our ring doorbell camera footage to see if we'd had an early morning visitor, and we had not. Are you intrigued by supernatural sights and sounds sent from heaven? I sure am!

In conjunction with my supernatural doorbell sound, one of my fellow authors had posted some pictures of a recent road trip. One of these photos really piqued my interest. When you examine the picture accompanying this week's blog post, what does it remind you of? At first blush, I thought it looked like a bird's profile picture.

_____

_____

_____

In prophetic symbolism, birds can have meanings commensurate with their specific species such as doves, hummingbirds, robins, etc. In general, birds represent good or evil spirits, The Holy Spirit (a dove), a church, or angels. Birds are also messengers of sorts.

Since there's usually not a doorbell without a door, it's instructive to examine the prophetic representation for a door first which is an entrance to something, faith, a time of transition (walking through a door), opportunity, Jesus Christ (Revelation 3:20 when Jesus stands at the door of our heart and knocks), mouth, or the work of God (1 Corinthians 16:9).

Doorbells speak of a call to prayer and time of communion with Jesus Christ, calling, or opportunity, arrival or looking for opportunities (if you are the one who rings the bell), and expectation or anticipation.

No Correlation

When writing this prophetic blog post, I deem there's no correlation between the supernatural sign in the sky via a cloud formation and my being awakened from a deep sleep by the sound of a doorbell. I just thought it would be fun in a spiritual sense to take a look at both of these and meditate upon them as God can speak to us in a myriad of ways including supernatural sights and sounds.

Sometimes Tied To His Word

There have been times in the past when I've had a supernatural "sound" encounter such as hearing three taps on my bedroom door, getting up, and finding no one there, then praying and asking the Lord if this is tied to His word in any way.

Tying together 4:06 a.m. on October 11, 2021, and consulting Psalm 40, verse 6, it reads, "Sacrifice and offering You did not desire, My **ears** you have opened. Burnt offering and sin offering You did not require." (Emphasis mine)

My ears, no pun intended, perked up when I read this verse since I'd heard the supernatural sound a few hours before this. Like the Psalmist has suggested in Psalm 63:1,

"O God, You *are* my God;
Early will I seek You;
My soul thirsts for You;
My flesh longs for You
In a dry and thirsty land
Where there is no water."

When seeking the Lord through His word earlier this morning, I came upon Psalm 40:6. This is also applicable since we are still in a drought in the west. There was an organized day of fasting and prayer this past weekend for the severe drought in our area. We are praying for abundant snowfall in the mountains this winter, so the spring run-off can fill our reservoirs.

God's Fingers At Work In The Big Blue Sky

Through childlike eyes, we can choose to view cloud formations as God's fingers at work in the big blue sky. When asking other people what the clouds look like, it's fascinating to hear their input. Some do not believe that cloud formations are formed by God and are heaven-sent, but I sure do!

Here are some additional pictures which were taken by my author friend. What do you see in each of them?

_____
_____
_____
_____
_____

Prophetic Insights For Daily Living

#1. It's been said that sometimes God gives us dreams and supernatural encounters when we're asleep as that's when our spirits and minds are more settled so we're able to receive what He's downloading to us. Have you ever experienced something like this? If not, pray and ask God to start giving you dreams during the night season. Record them in your prophetic journal. It can be most insightful and instructive to refer back to them to start connecting the dots to determine how and when God is speaking to you.

___

#2. If you're so inclined, study dreams and visions in the Bible. They appear in both the Old and New Testaments. Here's a weblink with some verses to help get you started.

http://www.ryanhart.org/bible-verses-about-dreams/

#3. Do some of you follow storms and keep a sharp eye on the weather? My daddy was a farmer, so this is something I learned from him. I don't follow storms per se, but I do enjoy glimpses of unique cloud formations.

#4. As you read my weekly blog post, study the prophetic symbolism, consider the supernatural doorbell sound, and look at the cloud formation, what comes to your mind or spirit?

_____
_____
_____
_____

#5. In 2020, one of my weekly blog posts focused upon dreams, dream decoding, and prophetic symbolism. Here's the link if you'd like to take a gander at it:

https://sheilaeismann.com/dream-interpretation/

There's a silly worldly saying, "Dream on!" Right now, it does seem quite appropriate. Here's wishing you a week filled with God's supernatural visitations and dreams sent from heaven above. Also, remember to look at the clouds every once in a while, and prepare to be amazed!

"For God may speak in one way, or in another,
Yet man does not perceive it.
In a dream, in a vision of the night,
When deep sleep falls upon men,
While slumbering on their beds,
Then He opens the ears of men,
And seals their instruction." (Job 33:14-16)

Sheila Eismann, Prophetic Seer, Blogger, Author, & Teacher, publishes her weekly blog posts endeavoring to encourage others through God's word. Her writings include teaching and instructions on how to apply prophetic insights for daily living.

Please subscribe to receive new blog posts on her website at www.sheilaeismann.com. by clicking the "Subscribe" button in the far upper right-hand corner of her Home webpage.

Sheila Eismann, Idaho native, author, and publisher of 15 books was raised on Sage Creek Farms in Southwestern Idaho. She pens inspirational and fictional books drawing upon her life experiences as a legal secretary, law firm office administrator, office manager for a national horse breed registry, and successful operator of a bookkeeping business. Midway through life, she discovered published authors and poets on both sides of her family. Eismann, a co-founder of ICAN (Idaho Creative Author's Network), speaks at Writer's and Women's Conferences. She endeavors to be an encourager with a sense of humor. Learn more about Sheila, read her weekly blog posts, and discover her books at www.sheilaeismann.com

Where to find Sheila Eismann online:

Email: **sheila@sheilaeismann.com**

Website: **www.sheilaeismann.com**

Facebook: **www.facebook.com/sheila.eismann**

Blog: **www.sheilaeismann.com**

LinkedIn: **Sheila Eismann**

Sheila's and Dan's books are also featured online in Sheila's Etsy shop: **www.etsy.com/shop/BooksbySheilaEismann**

Sheila invites you to check out her new website **www.sheilaeismann.com** and sign up to receive her blog posts in your email inbox. Please send her an email at **sheila@sheilaeismann.com** to say hello and to let her know what ministered to you the most in this workbook or your favorite blog post. Happy reading and studying!

OTHER BOOKS AVAILABLE FROM AUTHORS SHEILA EISMANN, DAN EISMANN & DESERT SAGE PRESS which can be purchased from: www.sheilaeismann.com or www.amazon.com.

Read and study with **Sheila Eismann,** Prophetic Author, Blogger, Speaker, and Teacher, in Volume 1 of her latest series titled ***Prophetic Insights for Daily Living.*** This **231-page** workbook can be used as a stand-alone devotional, individual Bible Study, or group study. Sheila describes various dreams, visions, prophetic words, and teachings she's been given by The Holy Spirit from August 2020 through December 2020 which are designed to help you grow in spiritual knowledge and the operation of The Holy Spirit gifts. Each entry includes questions, contemplation, reflection, or a call to action.

Read and study with **Sheila Eismann,** Prophetic Author, Blogger, Speaker, and Teacher, in Volume 2 of her latest series titled ***Prophetic Insights for Daily Living.*** This **234-page** workbook can be used as a stand-alone devotional, individual Bible Study or in a group study. Sheila describes various dreams, visions, prophetic words, and teachings she's been given by The Holy Spirit from January 2021 through May 2021 which are designed to help you grow in spiritual knowledge and the operation of The Holy Spirit gifts. Each entry includes questions, contemplation, reflection, or a call to action.

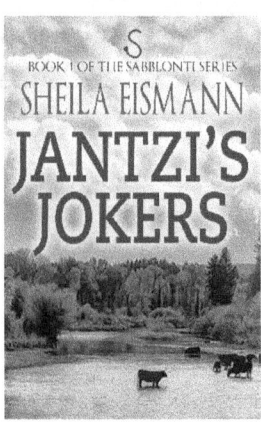

Western Fiction Book One of The Sabblonti Series, **Jantzi's Jokers**, features Jantzi Belle, the matriarch of the Sabblonti family, who has worked for decades to keep her cattle empire intact. Life takes a drastic turn when she receives a late-night visitor. The brief disappearance of her Last Will and Testament could complicate matters between her daughters, Stormy and Sarita. Stormy and her husband, Chet Castins, are struggling to work through the loss of their three children. Against all odds, drifter Wyn Moreland makes a bold move when he decides that Sarita is his beauty to rescue. The county veterinarian, Dr. Ben Shaw, is also vying for her affections. Will Wyn emerge as the winner? Just before the dawn of the New Year, revelations come forth regarding forgery, cattle rustling, and land exploitation. Will the Sabblonti Empire survive, and more importantly, who will control its reins?

The Sabblonti Saga accelerates in Book Two of the Series, **A Stormy Year**. Riding her high horse after inheriting the family fortune, Stormy Castins is determined to reinvent herself following her husband's accident. Blinded by jealousy, ambition, and naivety, she hires Less and Meg Alotto to oversee her vast high desert mountain domain. While Stormy is away, the cattle herd ends up in disarray.

Amidst the hot dry season, romance is blooming on several fronts despite a major showdown during a mid-summer celebration. The pesky Black Raven continues to wreak havoc at the most inopportune times.

Unable to overcome the vengeance which strikes by way of a mysterious range fire combined with the dire deeds of a cagey couple, the Sabblonti Ranch is in shambles just as Stormy starts to regain her senses. Humility is the prescription needed to open her eyes to realize what's truly important in life. The sparks from a belated holiday Rendevous set Chet and Stormy on their path to recovery.

Desperation explodes when heiress Stormy Sabblonti Castins calculates her dwindling fortune in Book 3 of the Sabblonti Series, **Love the Tie that Binds.** Is she capable of learning the painful lessons of having to rely upon someone and something other than inherited wealth? As her husband, Chet continues to heal from his near-fatal accident, tormenting shadows of The Black Raven lurk in the background.

These high desert hills are alive with blessed babies, enchanting engagements, skillful scavengers, sophisticated scoundrels, rich revelations, timeless treasures, and western weddings.

The Main Sabblonti Ranch house abounds with an unexpected marriage, childrens' voices, and Sir Shelton sporting his silver bell.

In a captivating story of courage, trust, and faithfulness, will Stormy still be tied in knots or find lasting love by the year's end?

Share the joys and sorrows of a mountain community in this swirling saga.

In this collection of true stories titled **Stirrings of The Spirit**, author Sheila Eismann invites you to walk with her family through several valleys en route to some mountain tops as they learned to rely on God in the most harrowing of circumstances.

Have you ever wondered why you were the last one to hear of THE big social event of the year? Well, wonder no longer after reading this e-book titled *Recognize Your Circles*! When volunteering for an organization years ago, author Sheila Eismann was introduced to the concept of "the circles of your life." Since the idea was so beneficial to her, she decided to share it with all of you.

Sheila F. Eismann

Straight from the Horse's Trough is a humorous read to assist the suburbanite or urbanite who desires to live a healthier lifestyle by growing his or her own food, but is faced with the challenge of a small space in which to do so. This e-book is chock full of how-to steps and includes pictures to remove the guesswork from the project.

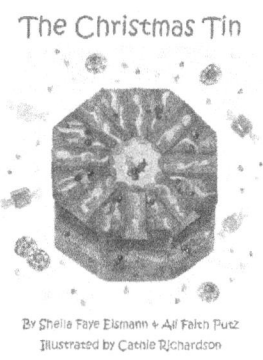

By Sheila Faye Eismann & Ajl Faith Putz
Illustrated by Cathie Richardson

The Christmas Tin is a most delightful read for the young at heart anytime during the year. This endearing book is based upon a true story featuring the older of the two authors when she was a young girl and conveys the timeless message that "love truly is the best gift of all." Children will especially enjoy all of the colorful illustrations contained within this treasure. There's a sugar cookie recipe included in the book and a helpful holiday suggestion for the kiddos to bless someone who's not expecting it at all!

FREEDOM IS YOUR DESTINY!

Daniel T. Eismann

Freedom is Your Destiny! Vietnam Veteran, Dan Eismann, using combat experiences to illustrate spiritual truths, invites you to take a journey with him as he presents a rock-solid strategy for not only fighting your spiritual battles but winning the all-important war. In the midst thereof, the most vital aspect is realizing you can experience freedom and become all that God has destined you to be!

Settle into your special reading spot; grab a cup of tea or your favorite meal. Be stirred as you read and ponder **Poetry Time, Volume One**; allow Sheila's words to encourage and heal.

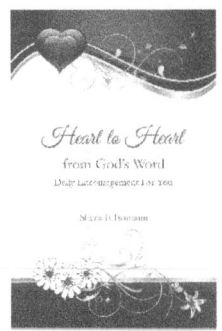

Everyone can use a little encouragement ~~ a dose of what is beneficial, ethical, and honorable. ***Heart to Heart From God's Word*** provides this for you. Penned with humor and wisdom, the daily tidbits are paired with Bible verses that convey life-changing principles which are designed for readers of all ages transcending cultures and continents. This devotional will challenge you to grow and fulfill your God-given destiny. It can also double as a prayer journal.

A Woman of Substance is a practical, interactive, and entertaining 12-week Bible study penned to help equip you to fulfill your God-given destiny and impact the culture for Jesus Christ at the same time. It can be used as a stand-alone study or devotional and works well in a group setting, too. It is designed for women ages junior high through adult.

ADDITIONAL NOTES & REFLECTIONS

Sheila Eismann

ADDITIONAL NOTES & REFLECTIONS

ADDITIONAL NOTES & REFLECTIONS

ADDITIONAL NOTES & REFLECTIONS

ADDITIONAL NOTES & REFLECTIONS

ADDITIONAL NOTES & REFLECTIONS

ADDITIONAL NOTES & REFLECTIONS

ADDITIONAL NOTES & REFLECTIONS

ADDITIONAL NOTES & REFLECTIONS

ADDITIONAL NOTES & REFLECTIONS

ADDITIONAL NOTES & REFLECTIONS

ADDITIONAL NOTES & REFLECTIONS

ADDITIONAL NOTES & REFLECTIONS

[i] Keesee, Ruby, Bible Studies for Women: The Gift of the Word of Knowledge (Caldwell, Idaho, 1990), PP. 1-4.

Keesee, Ruby, Bible Studies for Women: The Gift of the Word of Wisdom (Caldwell, Idaho, 1990), PP. 1-2.

[ii] Keesee, Ruby, Bible Studies for Women: The Gift of Discerning of Spirits, (Caldwell, Idaho, 1990), PP. 1-4.

[iii] Jeremiah 23:28.

[iv] AMG Dictionary – Old Testament, word 5030.

[v] Deuteronomy 18:18.

[vi] Jeremiah 20:8.

[vii] Jeremiah 20:9.

[viii] AMG Dictionary – Old Testament, word 2374.

[ix] AMG Dictionary – Old Testament, word 7200.

[x] Jeremiah 1:7, 9, 11, 12.

[xi] 1 Chronicles 29:29–30.

[xii] 2 Samuel 12:1–4.

[xiii] 2 Samuel 12:5.

[xiv] 2 Samuel 11:2–12:9.

[xv] Luke 1:5, 7, 11, 13, 16–17.

[xvi] 2 Chronicles 24:18–19.

[xvii] Acts 11:27–30.

[xviii] Acts 15:32.

[xix] Acts 13:1–3.

[xx] Jeremiah 1:9–10.

[xxi] House, Paul R. (2008) Note to Jeremiah 1:10. L. T. Dennis (Ex. Ed.), ESV Study Bible, English Standard Version. Wheaton, Ill.: Crossway Bibles.

[xxii] 1 Thessalonians 5:20–21.

[xxiii] 1 Corinthians 14:29–32.

[xxiv] Luke 2:36; Acts 2:17; 21:6.

www.ingramcontent.com/pod-product-compliance
Lightning Source LLC
Chambersburg PA
CBHW080637170426
43200CB00015B/2873